Vegan &
Vegetarian
Sushi Cookbook
for Beginners

VEGAN & VEGETARIAN

SUSHI
COOKBOOK
FOR BEGINNERS

50 Step-by-Step Recipes for Plant-Based Rolls

BRYAN SEKINE

ROCKRIDGE
PRESS

Interior and Cover Designer: Angie Chiu
Art Producer: Samantha Ulban
Editor: Gurvinder Singh Gandu
Production Editor: Jenna Dutton
Production Manager: Holly Haydash

Photography © 2021 Annie Martin, Cover and pp. ii, v, vi, ix, x, 12, 24, 56, 66, 80, 82, 112; Antonis Achilleos, pp. 25, 26, 67, 68. Food Styling by Lukas Grossman, Cover and pp. ii, v, vi, ix, x, 12, 24, 56, 66, 80, 82, 112. Illustrations by Angie Chiu.

Paperback ISBN: 978-1-63807-439-7
eBook ISBN: 978-1-63807-858-6
R0

TO MY WIFE, JENNI:
Thank you for encouraging me to chase my dreams and supporting me. I couldn't have eaten all this sushi without you!

CONTENTS

INTRODUCTION

My name is Bryan and I've been a professional sushi chef since 2008. I initially fell in love with sushi as a child when my mother took me to a traditional Japanese restaurant. I always enjoyed it when my mother made Japanese food for our family, and when I was old enough, she taught me how to cook my favorite dishes. After I graduated from high school, I went to college for IT, but found my passion for sushi while working part-time at a sushi restaurant.

In 2011, after working at two different restaurants and deciding to expand my knowledge of sushi even further, I started doing some online research and stumbled upon the term "sustainable sushi." After some surface-level research on what the sushi industry was doing, I became obsessed. I started researching fishing vessels, fishing methods, and population counts of the most popular species of seafood found in sushi. The more I researched, the more horrified I became.

I was unknowingly contributing to an industry that was killing our oceans in ways paralleled only by the oil industry. I felt awful. I thought what I was doing was horribly wrong. I thought about giving up . . . and for a while, I did. After a two-year hiatus, I decided that I would try to make a difference instead. A few close friends convinced me that I had a unique talent for teaching people how to roll sushi and that I could use that talent to create my own business. I started my website, Secrets of Sushi, and from that website came this book.

I wanted to write a book about vegan and vegetarian sushi because I want people to know that sushi is a lot more than just raw fish. Sushi is about attention to detail, perfecting each ingredient, and creating a symphony of flavor in every bite. You don't need seafood to make great-tasting sushi.

In addition to being favorable for our environment, eating vegan or vegetarian has a lot of health benefits. You probably already know a lot of them, which may be why you bought this book! I'm excited to share 40 vegan and vegetarian sushi recipes, as well as 10 recipes for sides and condiments.

My goal with this book is to teach you how to make the foods you love to eat at sushi restaurants, right at home. I want to show you how to make your favorite foods at any time, as well as entertain guests with your exciting new skills. You will learn many classic recipes, such as futomaki, avocado roll, miso soup, and Japanese ginger salad dressing, as well as several more imaginative recipes.

I know that sushi can seem like an intimidating cuisine to learn, but I have broken it down into step-by-step instructions so you can master the art of making sushi at home. This book provides recipes that you can master even if you're a beginner.

Let's get started!

CHAPTER 1

Vegan and Vegetarian Sushi

With this book as your guide, you will be able to make restaurant-quality sushi at home. Although the techniques for rolling sushi aren't as difficult as you might think, the secret to success lies in the details.

With that in mind, let's cover some basic techniques and learn why each detail is important. Each ingredient has a specific preparation method that brings out the best qualities of that ingredient. There are specialized pieces of equipment that make ingredient preparation easier, but this book was written so you won't need any significant investment other than your time and enthusiasm.

Sushi History and Culture

Contrary to popular belief, sushi includes more than just raw fish. The word *sushi* translates to "vinegared rice" and applies only to dishes that use sushi rice. *Sashimi* translates to "pierced fish" and can therefore apply only to raw fish. Although the two terms are often lumped together as describing the same cuisine, their history is quite different.

The earliest form of sushi was wildly different from the sushi we eat today. Sushi made its first appearance in Southeast Asia during the eighth century as a means of transporting fish. Originally called *narezushi* (fermented sushi), the initial style involved preserving fish by using fermented rice. When rice begins to ferment, it produces lactic acid, which, along with salt, causes a reaction that slows the growth of bacteria. This process was once thought to be a form of pickling and is the reason why the sushi kitchen is called a *tsuke-ba*, or "pickling place." The fish was gutted, salted, and wrapped in pickled rice for months before being consumed. The rice was for transportation purposes only; the fish was eaten, but the rice was discarded.

In the early 19th century, *makizushi* (sushi rolls), *nigirizushi* (fish on a ball of rice), and *chirashizushi* (seafood on a bowl of rice) were invented. This was the first time that seasoned rice and raw fish were added to the cuisine.

After World War II, rice and seafood were strictly rationed throughout Japan. During this period, the American occupation worked with the Japanese government to help revitalize the restaurant industry. This was both good and bad for sushi chefs: good because it inspired the expansion of ingredients from the traditional list, including an assortment of vegetables; bad because it limited the availability of rice and seafood to sushi chefs. The focus of sushi-making transitioned to the creation of a piece of art with a variety of perfectly portioned ingredients, where each could shine while supporting the others.

Jumping forward to the mid-1960s, the *uramaki* (inside-out roll) was created to persuade Western consumers to try raw fish. In the 1970s, flash-freezing technology allowed raw fish to be transported significantly farther than it had been previously. This sparked the spread of sushi worldwide and allowed cultures everywhere to influence its evolution.

Vegan and Vegetarian Sushi

Not only do vegan and vegetarian sushi belong to the early history of sushi, they remain a key component of the cuisine today.

This book is inspired by the numerous ways there are to enjoy the delicious flavors of vegetables and other vegan or vegetarian foods in sushi form. There are many types of vegan and vegetarian sushi recipes, and I have compiled my favorites in this book. I've also created several unique recipes for you to enjoy. The recipes emphasize the use of pickles, fresh vegetables, traditional seasonings, and unique sauces.

Food is an important part of anyone's culture. Food brings people together, creates memories, and gives you an immersive glimpse of history. When exploring a cuisine, it's important to understand the associated terminology. Here are some Japanese terms you'll come across in this book.

awase: Usually refers to a mixture of red miso and white miso

chirashi (scattered sushi): A form of sushi in which ingredients are placed on top of a bowl of sushi rice

daikon (big root): A large, long, white radish

dashi: A stock typically made with fish and kelp; widely used as a source of umami. In this book, shiitake mushrooms are used instead of fish.

edamame (stem bean): Steamed soybeans commonly served as an appetizer at Asian restaurants

furikake: A seasoning used on cooked rice, vegetables, and fish, commonly found in rice balls (*onigiri*) and containing dried fish

futomaki (fat roll): One of the largest forms of sushi

gobo (greater burdock): Pickled burdock root

gunkan maki (war boat sushi): A ball of sushi rice wrapped with seaweed and topped with ingredients that don't work inside a sushi roll

gyoza (dumpling): Chinese dumplings, also called "pot stickers," typically filled with minced meat and vegetables

hangiri or handai: A wooden, flat-bottom bowl or tub used in the final steps of preparing rice for sushi—cooling and seasoning

hosomaki (thin roll): One of the earliest forms of sushi with typically only one ingredient inside, and seaweed on the outside; commonly cut into six pieces

inarizushi or inari (fox sushi): A marinated tofu pouch stuffed with sushi rice; considered a favorite dish of the Shinto fox spirit

kombu: An edible kelp harvested and dried for its strong umami flavor; one of the main ingredients in dashi

maki (sushi roll): This term distinguishes rolled sushi from all other forms of sushi and can include all the variations of sushi rolls

makisu: The bamboo rolling mat used to make maki

musubi (to tie or bring together): A Hawaiian snack of grilled Spam on rice, wrapped in nori

nigiri (gripped sushi): A ball of rice and slice of fish pressed together by hand

nori or sushi nori (seaweed): Commonly refers to toasted seaweed used for sushi

oshinko (fragrant dish): Refers to many Japanese pickled vegetables, but most commonly used for pickled daikon radishes

oshizushi (pressed sushi): One of the earliest forms of sushi, *oshizushi* can be pressed from between two hours to several days, depending on the ingredients

santoku (three virtues): A modern Japanese knife based on the Western chef's knife

shoyu: Broadly used for Japanese-style soy sauce; typically, shoyu is lighter in color and made with only fermented soybeans, wheat, salt, and water

tamago: "Egg" in Japanese; also a type of sweet omelet used in making sushi

temaki (hand roll): A style of sushi that resembles an ice-cream cone

temari (ball sushi): A symmetrically round ball of rice and fish

tobiko (flying fish eggs): Roe specifically from a flying fish; the type of roe most commonly found in sushi

togarashi: A spice mixture; the most common form is *shichimi togarashi*, or "seven spice," containing chili powder, pepper, roasted orange peel, sesame seeds, ginger, seaweed, and poppy seeds.

umami: Widely regarded as the fifth flavor—savoriness

uramaki (inside-out roll): A roll with rice on the outside, commonly cut into eight pieces

wakame: An edible brown seaweed

Sushi-Making Equipment

In this section I cover the few essential pieces of equipment you will need to make sushi at home. There is also a list of nice-to-have items that, although not necessary, can make the process a little easier. Most of these tools can be found online or at Asian supermarkets, and they are not expensive.

Essentials

Makisu (bamboo sushi mat): This mat is crucial for making sushi rolls. You should purchase one with flat slats for easier rolling and be sure never to put it in the dishwasher. I recommend wrapping the makisu in plastic wrap before using it to roll sushi. This will keep the mat clean and make rolling sushi much easier. If you have a hard plastic makisu, you will not need to wrap it in plastic wrap, and, depending on the manufacturer's recommendation, you may be able to wash it in a dishwasher.

Rice paddle: Seasoning sushi rice is the single most important step in making sushi. A rice paddle makes seasoning your sushi rice much easier. I recommend using a plastic paddle rather than wood or bamboo because the rice won't stick to plastic as easily.

Sauce bottles: The presentation of food is important. The best way to make sauce look appetizing with sushi is to use a sauce bottle. These can be new or recycled sauce bottles (sriracha bottles are great). Sauce bottles are also the preferred way to store sauces after they are made.

Sharp knife: You don't need a sushi-specific knife as long as the knife you are using is razor sharp. The sharper the knife, the easier it will be to slice your sushi. I recommend starting with a thin, short chef's knife that is easy to maintain and easy to sharpen. Remember to always keep your knife sharp!

Nice-to-Haves

Cutting board: Consider upgrading your cutting board for sushi-making. Most cutting boards are either plastic or wood, which tend to get scratches deep enough to trap bacteria. The boards also tend to chip, discolor, or warp over time. I recommend a rubber-compound, antimicrobial cutting board. These boards can be resurfaced by sanding and are resistant to chipping, warping, and discoloration.

Handai: This wooden tub can take average sushi rice and turn it into superb sushi rice by absorbing the excess water and vinegar that the rice doesn't soak up. This item tends to be more expensive than most people want to spend for homemade sushi, but if you are a sushi aficionado, or going for professional-grade sushi, a handai is an excellent piece of equipment.

Oshizushi press: This small wooden box is designed to press sushi together to make oshizushi. This tool is helpful because oshizushi needs to be pressed for at least an hour and will allow you to conveniently set a heavy object on your sushi while you prepare other ingredients.

Rice cooker: Rice cookers ensure perfectly cooked sushi rice every single time. You can cook rice in a pot on the stove, but a high-quality rice cooker will avoid the hassle of keeping an eye on the rice, overcooking or undercooking it, and uncertainty about the consistency. A good rice cooker also allows you to prepare other ingredients while the rice is cooking. Choose a rice cooker with a stainless-steel pot or an aluminum pot if your rice cooker supports induction heating.

Whetstone: Whetstones are needed only if you have purchased a Japanese knife. These come in various grits, or coarseness, but you will need at least two to sharpen your sushi knife (preferably 1,000 grit and 6,000 grit). Whetstones are the only way to properly sharpen a single-bevel knife and they require a specific technique to use and store.

A sushi knife is an extension of the sushi chef's hand and a reflection of their attention to detail. A good knife will make every cut easier and more precise, and produce higher quality results. A good knife can make a world of difference, but it doesn't have to be expensive; almost any knife will do as long as it's sharp.

Although you may not need a brand-new knife to slice vegetables, you should use a knife that is razor sharp, relatively thin, and preferably shorter than nine inches. The thinner the vegetable is cut, the more surface area is exposed to air, enhancing the flavor. Thinner blades are simply more capable of making thinner slices.

There are several differences between Western knives and Japanese knives. Japanese knives are single-bevel, made from high-carbon steel, and are sharpened in the opposite direction from Western knives. Japanese knives should always be washed and sharpened by hand. The best method for sharpening your sushi knife is with a whetstone, but you could also go to a professional knife sharpener.

I have two recommendations for a sushi knife: the Usuba and the Santoku, each of which has special qualities for slicing vegetables. If you'd like to read more about these knives and view step-by-step instructions on how to sharpen your sushi knife, visit my website at SecretsOfSushi.com.

Fresh Ingredients

In this section I introduce the essential fresh ingredients needed for vegan and vegetarian sushi. Most are easily found in large supermarkets, but some varieties may be available only in grocery stores that prioritize produce.

Asparagus: Asparagus is best used when the stalks are thin and briefly blanched. They provide a rich flavor, bright color, and subtle texture inside sushi. This vegetable pairs perfectly with Vegetarian Miso Mayonnaise (page 106) or lemon juice.

Avocados: Choosing the right avocado to use in sushi is all about the consistency and ripeness. Ripe avocados provide the perfect amount of savory, creamy flavor. To test for ripeness, peel off the stem nub. If the avocado is green underneath, it is ready to use. If it's brown underneath, the avocado is past its prime and shouldn't be used in sushi. Avocados should be peeled by hand (never scooped out with a spoon) to help prevent oxidation.

Bell peppers: The color of bell peppers indicates how long they were left to mature on the plant. All bell peppers start off green and then turn yellow, orange, and finally red. Green bell peppers have a more bitter flavor, whereas red bell peppers provide the sweetest flavor. The color of the bell pepper to use will vary depending on the flavor profile you want for your sushi.

Cucumbers: Cucumbers bring a refreshing flavor and crisp texture to sushi. Japanese, English, or American slicing cucumbers (also known as "slicers") are the most commonly used varieties for sushi. Japanese and English cucumbers are preferred because they contain fewer seeds and less cucurbitacin, the bitter compound that causes gas buildup in the stomach.

Mushrooms: Several varieties of mushrooms can be used in sushi, but I prefer king oyster mushrooms. They work incredibly well as a vegan substitute for shellfish—especially scallops and shrimp. Oyster mushrooms are easy to tempura-fry and tend to absorb whatever flavors you cook them with.

Scallions: Scallions should be thinly sliced to bring out their strong, zesty flavor and aroma. If you want a more subtle flavor, rinse scallions under cold water and allow them to air dry before storing or using.

Sweet potatoes: Orange and purple sweet potatoes work best for sushi. They are highly nutritious and very versatile. Sweet potatoes for sushi are most often baked, roasted, or deep-fried.

Tofu: Firm or extra-firm tofu tends to work best in sushi. Tofu can be pan-seared, deep-fried, stir-fried, or used in miso soup. Tofu is bland by itself, but it's great at absorbing other flavors.

Pantry Ingredients

Here are the essential nonperishable ingredients needed for making vegan and vegetarian sushi:

Nori sheets: Nori sheets should be toasted and unflavored, and they should stay crisp and dry when stored at home. Most packs of nori come in full sheets or half sheets, and the packages are color-coded to signify the quality of the nori. From highest to lowest: gold, silver, blue, and green. Not every package abides by this system, but almost every gold-level nori package will advertise that fact.

Rice wine vinegar: Without this ingredient you won't be able to make sushi rice! Rice wine vinegar, also called rice vinegar, should be fairly easy to find in most supermarkets. Be sure to buy only the variety that contains no added sugar or salt, as you will add your own amounts of each.

Sushi rice: There are tons of different types of rice in the world, but the type that works best for sushi is short-grain white rice. Medium-grain white rice can be used in a pinch if short grain is not available. Rice is covered in more detail in the next chapter.

Sauces, Wasabi, and Pickled Ginger

Mirin: Mirin, often referred to as a sweet cooking wine, has a thick consistency. Although you might think that mirin and sake could be used interchangeably, mirin has its own distinct flavor.

Sake: Rice wine is not just delicious to drink, it's also an essential component of Japanese cuisine. Many sauces used for sushi call for sake or "cooking wine," and the two are not necessarily interchangeable. Cooking wine should not be consumed as a beverage, and sake should not be used for cooking unless it's unflavored and filtered.

Soy sauce: The only type of soy sauce that should be used for sushi is shoyu (see page 4). You can substitute tamari—gluten-free soy sauce—if you are allergic or have a gluten allergy.

Ponzu Sauce: This is a special soy sauce that is blended with citrus juice. Traditionally made with yuzu, a type of Japanese lemon, ponzu is a delightfully refreshing alternative to conventional soy sauce and it is simple to make at home.

Wasabi: This is a quintessential accompaniment in Western sushi restaurants, but not nearly as common in Japan. In fact, most Japanese sushi bars won't put wasabi on your plate at all. What we see as wasabi is most often horseradish mixed with mustard powder and food coloring. Real wasabi must be freshly grated within minutes of eating because it oxidizes so quickly that it loses flavor. Wasabi is hard to grow, finicky to transport, and has a surprisingly short shelf life.

If you would like to try real wasabi at home, I recommend buying a wasabi rhizome online along with a sharkskin grating board, also known as a *chojiro*. Peel off the skin and gently grate the rhizome in a circular motion. Once you have a pea-size amount, collect the wasabi and put it on a soy sauce dish for immediate use. Keep in mind that wasabi and soy sauce should never be mixed!

Pickled ginger: Pickled ginger is another sushi accompaniment that is used differently in Western sushi restaurants and in Japanese restaurants. In Japan, pickled ginger is eaten only between bites of nigiri or before eating a new sushi roll, because it is meant to be a palate cleanser. Typically, the guest would place a single piece of pickled ginger on their tongue and let it rest inside their mouth for a few moments before chewing and eating it. Letting the ginger rest on the tongue maximizes the flavor-cleansing effect.

Although many Westerners place pickled ginger directly on a piece of sushi before eating it, it's considered counterproductive because it will reduce the subtle flavors you could be tasting.

Serving Sushi

Eating sushi can be a casual or highly formal experience. Although many sushi restaurants in North America and Europe don't strictly follow the traditional etiquette, I believe it is important to understand, practice, and pay respect to the culture by demonstrating proper sushi etiquette. This applies to chefs as well as guests.

Plating arrangement makes a huge impact on how people perceive food. If the food is presented well, it will be perceived as tasting better. Eating should be a complete experience, not just about how the food tastes; it should activate all your senses to build an unforgettable meal.

When serving sushi at home there are a few key things to remember:

* Sushi should be presented neatly with a balance of sharp lines and curves.

* The best plates are those with minimal design and consistent coloring.

* White plates work well for highlighting the color of the sushi.

* Avoid overcrowding a plate; instead, embrace the empty space.

* If sauce is served on top of a roll, make sure it does not run onto another piece of sushi or another roll.

* Avoid using the same saucing technique for every roll. Some rolls look better with the sauce drizzled on top (in a zigzag line) whereas others look better with dots of sauce.

* Place toppings intentionally! Don't scatter toppings all over the plate; instead, use chopsticks or food tweezers to precisely place the toppings on each piece. Don't sprinkle too much on top of the roll and throw the flavor of the bite off balance.

* Ask your guests if they have any food allergies, and present any potentially problematic sushi dishes on a separate plate/platter.

* Each guest should have a small plate, soy sauce dish, napkin, and pair of chopsticks. The chopsticks should rest on the soy sauce dish and lie parallel to the edge of the table. Don't fill the soy sauce dish; let your guest decide if they want soy sauce.

* Offer low-sodium shoyu as well as regular shoyu.

* When serving drinks, it is customary for the host to refill their guests' drinks.

Enjoying Sushi

Following traditional etiquette when eating sushi is not only polite, it also allows you to savor nuances of flavor you may never have noticed before.

* Although using chopsticks is a classic way to eat sushi, you may use your fingers to eat nigiri.

* If you want to dip nigiri into shoyu, always dip the topping, not the rice, into the sauce. This helps keep the rice together instead of falling apart in the soy sauce dish.

* To get a piece of sushi from another person's plate, grab the piece with the ends of the chopsticks that you are holding, not the ends that go into your mouth.

* Never pass food from chopsticks to chopsticks, as this closely resembles an important part of a Japanese funeral ceremony.

* Avoid putting wasabi in your soy sauce dish. Instead, place the desired amount of wasabi on your piece of sushi before dipping it in soy sauce.

* Ginger should be eaten only between bites and not on top of sushi or dipped in soy sauce. Dipping ginger in soy sauce is the equivalent of squirting ketchup directly into your mouth when eating french fries.

CHAPTER 2

Setting Up for Sushi Success

Over the past five years I have taught hundreds of people how to make sushi at home, and one thing became clear: Making proper sushi rice was the single most common challenge people had. The first half of this chapter is dedicated to teaching you how to make perfect sushi rice every time.

The Importance of Sushi Rice

Sushi rice is the most important part of making sushi. The perfectly seasoned rice is stored at room temperature and passes health inspections only because of the precisely lowered pH, which makes the rice too acidic for bacteria to grow on.

Most people believe getting sick from eating sushi is because of bad fish, when really it is far more likely that you ate bad rice. Rice is a carbohydrate, which bacteria can break down into sugar at a much faster rate than it can vegetables or meat. If you do not thoroughly and correctly season sushi rice, it will start to grow bacteria within a few hours.

The seasoning for sushi rice consists of rice wine vinegar, sugar, and salt. These ingredients work together not just to flavor the rice but also to help preserve it. Sushi chefs often refer to this mixture as *su*, but that term could also simply refer to vinegar. The word *su-shi* was created from this seasoning and the Japanese word for cooked rice: *meshi*. Sushi literally translates to "vinegar rice."

This is the recipe for su, or rice seasoning:

4 cups rice wine vinegar
2 cups sugar
1 cup salt

1. In a large pot over medium heat, combine the vinegar, sugar, and salt.

2. Stir occasionally until the salt and sugar dissolve. Do not let it come to a boil.

3. Pour the mixture into a glass jar to cool.

Su does not need to be refrigerated as long as it's stored in a sealed container. It should be used only after it has cooled to room temperature.

White Rice

Short- or medium-grain rice is ideal for sushi because it has the right amount of starch to create the best consistency. Long-grain rice, such as jasmine or basmati, doesn't contain enough starch to stick together.

Before cooking rice, wash it. This removes any excess starch created during the milling process. To wash rice, fill a pot with the desired amount of rice and cover it completely with cold water. Gently swirl the rice with one hand in a circular motion, being careful not to break the grains. When the water is milky white, pour it out and refill the pot with cold water. Repeat until the water is significantly less cloudy.

Traditionally, sushi chefs washed their rice until the water turned completely clear. This usually took 25 to 30 washes, which, in my experience, doesn't produce a noticeable difference in taste or texture. I wash rice three times per one cup of rice.

I prefer to use a rice cooker for consistency, speed, and ease of use, but the steps to make sushi rice on a stovetop follow as well. For both cooking methods, keep these tips in mind:

* Don't open the lid while the rice is cooking. This will release the steam that is vital for properly cooked sushi rice.
* Don't worry about soaking the rice prior to cooking unless you are cooking the rice on a stovetop.
* Season the rice while still hot, so the rice can absorb more seasoning as it cools.
* Be gentle when removing rice from the pot. Rice is at its most fragile when it comes out of the pot, and it's important not to smash the grains.

Tamanishiki short-grain rice is my favorite, but any short- or medium-grain white rice will do.

Making Sushi Rice

IN A RICE COOKER:

1. After washing the rice, place the pot inside the rice cooker and add 1 cup of water for each cup of rice. Use the same measuring cup for the rice and the water.

2. Close the lid on the rice cooker and press the button down to the "Cook" position.

3. When the rice cooker has popped back to the "Warm" position, remove the rice pot and dump the rice onto your seasoning container (preferably a handai, but any large wooden cutting board will do). Use a rice paddle to gently remove any rice stuck to the pot.

ON THE STOVETOP:

1. After washing the rice, put it in a heavy-bottomed pot. Add 25 percent more water than the amount of rice (e.g., for 2 cups of rice, add 2½ cups of water). Allow the rice to soak in the pot for 20 to 30 minutes.

2. Place a tight-fitting lid on the pot and bring the water to a boil over medium heat. You should be able to hear the water boiling without removing the lid, but if not, it's okay to lift the lid (briefly) to check.

3. When the water has come to a boil, reduce the heat to low and cook the rice for 12 minutes. Do not remove the lid.

4. After 12 minutes, lift the lid briefly to check if the water has completely boiled off. If not, cook for a few more minutes. If the water has boiled off, remove the pot from the stovetop and let the rice steam for an additional 10 minutes.

5. Dump the rice onto your seasoning container. Use a rice paddle to gently scrape out any rice stuck to the pot.

SEASONING RICE:

1. Gather the rice into a large mound.

2. Pour the su mixture (see page 14) over the rice paddle and shake the paddle from side to side. Use 2 tablespoons of su per 1 cup of uncooked rice.

3. Use the rice paddle to gently spread out the seasoned rice and allow it to cool.

4. Once the rice has stopped steaming, flip the rice over in small sections. Allow the rice to cool on this side as well.

5. After the rice has been flipped several times and is cool, scoop the rice into a sealed container until you are ready to assemble your sushi.

Brown Rice

Brown rice is often considered to be healthier than white rice; however, it doesn't contain the same levels of starch as white rice and therefore doesn't bind together as easily. For this reason, I recommend using brown sushi rice only in chirashi bowls, temaki, and gunkan maki.

Because brown rice still has the husk and bran attached to each grain, it takes significantly longer to soak and cook. Rinse brown rice two or three times per pot.

I prefer using a pressure cooker over a rice cooker for brown rice because it significantly reduces the cooking time.

Making Brown Sushi Rice

ON THE STOVETOP:

1. After washing the rice, put it in a heavy-bottomed pot. Add water using a 2:3 ratio (e.g., 2 cups of rice to 3 cups of water). **Allow the rice to soak in the pot for 2 to 3 hours before you begin cooking.**

2. Place a tight-fitting lid on the pot and bring the water to a boil over medium heat. You should be able to hear the water boiling without removing the lid, but if not, it's okay to lift the lid (briefly) to check.

3. When the water has come to a boil, reduce the heat to low and cook the rice for 17 to 20 minutes. Do not remove the lid.

4. After at least 17 minutes, lift the lid briefly to check if the water has completely boiled off. If not, cook the rice for a few more minutes. If the water has boiled off, remove the pot from the stovetop and let the rice steam for an additional 5 to 10 minutes.

5. Dump the rice onto your seasoning container. Use a rice paddle to gently scrape out any rice stuck to the pot.

IN AN ELECTRIC PRESSURE COOKER:

1. After washing the rice, put it in the pressure cooker pot. Add 25 percent more water than the amount of rice (e.g., for 2 cups of rice, add 2½ cups of water).

2. Close the lid on the pressure cooker and cook on "High" pressure for 15 minutes. Let the pressure cooker do a full, natural release of pressure.

3. Once the pressure cooker has released its pressure, remove the lid and carefully dump the rice onto your seasoning container. Use a rice paddle to carefully scrape out any rice in the bottom of the pot.

TROUBLESHOOTING RICE

Here are a few common problems that might arise when cooking sushi rice, along with a solution for each:

Rice is too soft and mushy

Typically, this means there was too much water used to cook the rice. This applies both to cooking rice on the stovetop and in a rice cooker.

Rice is too hard and chewy

This problem usually comes from not using enough water in the rice cooker or pot.

Rice doesn't stick together

This happens when the wrong type of rice was used or when the rice wasn't seasoned with su.

Making too much or too little rice

One cup of uncooked rice should make three uramaki or five to six pieces of nigiri. I wouldn't suggest trying to cook less than 1 cup of rice at a time.

Rice is too sticky and sticks to your hands

This is typically not an issue with the rice itself but rather with how much water was on your hands before handling the rice. Anytime you touch sushi rice, you want to make sure your hands are slightly wet. Dip two fingers into a small bowl of water and transfer the water to your opposite hand. Rub your hands together until they are glossy, but not dripping with water.

Preparing Vegetables and Other Common Items

In this section I provide an overview of the most common ingredients used in rolls and how to prepare them. This section can be referenced for the subsequent recipes.

ASPARAGUS

1. Cut the bottom off each stalk, if needed. You'll know to do this if the asparagus stalks feel hard and have the consistency of a stick.

2. Blanch the asparagus by putting it in boiling water for 3 minutes and then immediately transferring it to a bowl of ice water to stop the cooking process.

3. Pat the asparagus dry using paper towels, and store in the refrigerator.

AVOCADOS

1. Slice in half, lengthwise, and remove the pit by chopping a knife into it and twisting the knife.

2. Carefully remove the pit from the knife and discard it. Peel each half of the avocado by hand (this helps keep the avocado from browning as quickly).

3. Use the tip of the knife to "draw a line" through the avocado. This helps prevent the thin slices from sticking to the knife. Place the tip of the knife on the cutting board, above the avocado, and draw it back through the avocado. Make sure to keep the knife at the same angle throughout the entire process. Slice the avocado into ⅛-inch-thick slices.

4. Place the avocado slices on a plate and cover until ready to use.

CARROTS

1. Peel and cut off the ends. Cut the carrots in half across and then cut those halves in half again lengthwise.

2. Cut the carrots into sticks about 3 inches long.

3. You can blanch the carrot sticks for a softer texture and more flavor, or leave them raw for more crunch and higher nutrient levels.

4. To blanch carrots, bring a pot of water to a boil. Boil the carrots for 3 minutes and then immediately transfer them to a bowl of ice water to stop the cooking process.

5. Dry the carrots and store them in a covered container until ready to use.

CUCUMBERS

1. Peel completely and slice off the ends. Cut in half horizontally to make two round halves.

2. Set each half on its smallest end and make four slices around the seeds to create four cucumber panels. Set the panels on a few paper towels, cover with more paper towels, and let them drain for 10 minutes.

3. Remove the paper towels and slice each panel into ⅛-inch-thick pieces.

RED BELL PEPPERS

1. Slice off the top and bottom. Remove the seeds by hand and discard them.

2. Slice the three or four sides of the pepper into flat sections.

3. Slice each section into thin strips, about ⅛ inch thick.

SCALLIONS

1. Wash and slice at a 30-degree angle. Try to make the slices as thin as possible. Note: The recipes in this book utilize the green parts only.

2. For a strong flavor, you can stop at this step and store the scallions in a sealed container. If you would like a more subtle flavor, rinse the scallions in cold water using a colander. Allow to dry before storing in a sealed container.

SWEET POTATOES

1. Preheat the oven to 425°F.

2. Peel and cut into slabs about ½ inch thick. After the first cut, you can rotate the potato so the flat side is facedown on the cutting board. Continue cutting slabs until you have sliced all the potato.

3. Slice the slabs into ½-inch-wide strips. They should resemble french fries.

4. Toss the strips into a bowl and sprinkle them with cornstarch. Pour 2 tablespoons of olive oil into a separate bowl, then add the lightly coated strips and toss them in the oil. Make sure there are no dry spots of cornstarch on the strips.

5. Bake the potato strips for 30 minutes. Flip the strips halfway through the cooking process to ensure they cook evenly.

About the Recipes

The recipes in this book will help you build a foundation for making delicious vegan and vegetarian sushi. All the recipes are suitable for beginners, but they progress in complexity throughout the book.

At any time, refer to page 14 for how to cook sushi rice and page 19 for instructions on preparing ingredients. In the ingredient lists, "sushi rice" means cooked and seasoned rice.

Labels at the top of each recipe indicate the type of sushi. If the recipe has eggs in it, you'll see the "contains egg" text and an icon:

🥚 CONTAINS EGG

Here are the labels (see pages 3 and 4 for definitions):

CHIRASHI	MUSUBI
FUTOMAKI	NIGIRI
GUNKAN MAKI	OSHIZUSHI
HOSOMAKI	TEMAKI
INARI	TEMARI
MAKI	URAMAKI

Maki *(Rolls)* and Temaki *(Hand Rolls)*

FUTOMAKI ROLL

MAKES 3 ROLLS OR 36 PIECES ✳ PREP TIME: 25 MINUTES

The futomaki is one of my favorite vegetarian sushi rolls. This roll is named after a style rather than a specific recipe. The roll is considered traditional because it uses *tamago* (sweet Japanese omelet) and *gobo* (pickled burdock root). Although some people prefer to use gobo for its distinctive pickled flavor, you can use blanched carrots instead. ⊖ CONTAINS EGG

3 full sheets nori

2 cups sushi rice

¼ block Tamago (page 111 or store-bought), sliced

6 gobo pieces or sliced blanched carrots

½ cucumber, sliced

10 to 12 blanched asparagus stalks

½ avocado, sliced

Garlic Mayonnaise (page 107) (optional)

Sesame seeds (optional)

1. Place a bamboo mat on the countertop and set a bowl of water beside it.

2. Place a full sheet of nori (or two half sheets side by side) rough-side-up on the mat.

3. Dip one hand into the bowl of water and rub your hands together. Your hands should be glossy wet, but not dripping with water. Spread one-third of the rice across the nori in a layer 2 to 3 grains deep, leaving a ½-inch clear border at the top of the nori.

4. Place one-third of the tamago, gobo, cucumber, asparagus, and avocado across the center of the rice, making sure that you are using consistent coverage of each ingredient.

CONTINUED

5. Tuck your thumbs under the bamboo mat, hold the ingredients with your fingers, and roll the mat up and over the ingredients until the bottom edge of the nori touches the bare rice.

6. Give the roll a firm squeeze to make sure there is no excess air inside the roll. You should be able to slowly remove your hands from the mat without having the roll come undone. If any ingredients are poking out, use your fingertips to tuck them back in.

7. Dip your fingers into the water again and transfer just enough to dampen the bare strip of nori. Continue rolling forward until the damp seaweed is pressed against the dry exterior side of the seaweed.

8. Repeat steps 2 through 7 to make two more rolls.

9. Slice each futomaki in half, using long, sawing motions. Next, slice each half in half again. Finally, slice each piece into thirds for a total of 12 pieces.

10. Drizzle with garlic mayonnaise and sprinkle sesame seeds on top (if using).

CUCUMBER ROLL

MAKES 4 SMALL ROLLS OR 24 PIECES ✳ PREP TIME: 15 MINUTES

The cucumber roll is a perfect recipe for anyone new to making sushi. This Hosomaki (thin) style of rolling sushi is traditional in Japan and most single-vegetable recipes will be rolled in this fashion.

4 half sheets nori
2 cups sushi rice
1 cucumber, sliced

1. Place a bamboo mat on the countertop and set a bowl of water beside it.

2. Place a half sheet of nori on the mat, with the smooth side of the nori facedown and the longest edge parallel to the bottom edge of the mat.

3. Dip one hand into the water and rub your hands together. Your hands should be glossy wet, but not dripping. Spread ½ cup of rice across the nori in a layer 2 to 3 grains deep, leaving a ½-inch clear border at the top of the nori. Arrange one-fourth of the cucumber in a straight line across the center of the rice-covered portion.

4. Tuck your thumbs under the bamboo mat, hold the cucumber with your fingers, and roll the mat up and over the cucumber until the bottom edge of the nori touches the rice above the cucumber.

5. Give the roll a firm squeeze to make sure there is no excess air inside. You should be able to slowly remove your hands from the mat without having the roll come undone. If any ingredients are poking out, use your fingertips to tuck them in.

6. Dip your fingers into the water again and transfer just enough to dampen the bare strip of nori. Continue rolling forward until the damp nori is covered. Give the roll one firm squeeze to seal.

7. Repeat steps 2 through 6 to make three more rolls.

8. Slice each roll in half through the middle, then cut the halves into thirds.

AVOCADO ROLL

MAKES 4 SMALL ROLLS OR 24 PIECES ✳ PREP TIME: 15 MINUTES

The avocado roll is another great single-ingredient recipe to help you learn the fundamental sushi-rolling technique. This recipe uses the futomaki style of rolling sushi, but uses only a half sheet of seaweed. Although the roll might seem too large at first, it will be sliced into six pieces, making each bite more manageable.

4 half sheets nori
2 cups sushi rice
2 avocados, sliced

1. Place a bamboo mat on the countertop and set a bowl of water beside it.

2. Place a half sheet of nori on the mat, with the smooth side of the nori facedown and the longest edge parallel to the cotton strings.

3. Dip one hand into the water and rub your hands together. Your hands should be glossy wet, but not dripping. Spread ½ cup of rice across the nori in a layer 2 to 3 grains deep, leaving a clear ½-inch border at the top of the nori.

4. Stack a ½-inch-thick line of avocado across the center of the rice-covered portion.

5. Tuck your thumbs under the bamboo mat, hold the avocado with your fingers, and roll the mat up and over the avocado until the bottom edge of the nori touches the rice above the avocado.

6. Give the roll a firm squeeze to make sure there is no excess air inside the roll. You should be able to slowly remove your hands from the mat without having the roll come undone.

7. Take 5 to 10 grains of rice and spread them on the bare portion of nori. Use your thumbs to smash the rice until they form a paste-like consistency.

8. Continue rolling everything forward until the rice paste is covered. Give the roll one firm downward press to seal.

9. Repeat steps 2 through 8 to make three more rolls.

10. Futomaki is traditionally cut into 12 pieces, but because this recipe is made with a half sheet, cut each roll into six pieces. Make sure your knife is clean, damp, and sharp. Slice each roll in half through the middle, then cut the halves into thirds.

TIP: To get extra-clean cuts, wipe your knife with a damp towel between each slice.

DAGOBAH ROLL

MAKES 4 ROLLS OR 32 PIECES ✳ **PREP TIME: 35 MINUTES** ✳ **COOK TIME: 20 MINUTES**

Seaweed salad has a unique texture and boasts a multitude of health benefits. Seaweed in general is high in iodine and antioxidants, and is believed to slow down the rate at which you feel hungry. The wakame salad is already cooked and only needs enough time in the oil to cook the tempura batter. I use peanut oil for tempura-frying because it has a high smoke point. In the case of peanut allergies, you can substitute canola oil anywhere peanut oil is used. ⊘ **CONTAINS EGG**

Peanut oil

1 egg, beaten

1 cup ice-cold water

1 cup all-purpose
flour, sifted

3 ice cubes

8 ounces seaweed salad
(wakame)

4 half sheets nori

2 cups sushi rice

1 (3-ounce) block
cream cheese

1 cucumber, sliced

1 avocado, sliced

1. Fill a skillet with 1 inch of oil and place the pan on high heat. Line a plate with paper towels.

2. While the oil is heating, prepare the tempura batter. In a medium bowl, combine the egg and water. Mix really well and then add the flour. Stir the flour in, but don't whisk it; the batter should be significantly clumpy. Add the ice and store the batter in the refrigerator until the oil is hot enough.

3. When the oil reaches at least 375°F, take one-fourth of the seaweed salad, dip it into the batter, swirl to evenly coat, and carefully add it to the oil. The goal is to have the seaweed create a "net" long enough to cover a sushi roll. When the batter has turned golden yellow, use tongs to transfer the tempura wakame to the paper towel–lined plate or a drying rack.

4. Put a bamboo mat on the countertop and set a bowl of water beside it.

5. Place a half sheet of nori on the mat, with the smooth side of the nori facedown and the longest edge parallel to the bottom edge of the mat.

6. Dip one hand into the water and rub your hands together. Your hands should be glossy wet, but not dripping. Spread ½ cup of rice across the entire sheet of nori in a layer 2 to 3 grains deep. Flip the rice and nori mat over so the rice is facedown.

7. Pinch off one-third of the cream cheese and form a 1-inch line of it across the center of the nori. Take 2 or 3 cucumber slices and place them against the cream cheese on the side farthest from you. Then lay 2 or 3 slices of avocado against the cream cheese on the side closest to you. The order of ingredients is important.

8. Tuck your thumbs under the mat, hold the ingredients with your fingers, and roll the bamboo mat up and over the ingredients until you reach the end of the mat.

9. Give the roll a firm squeeze to make sure there is no excess air inside the roll. You should be able to slowly remove your hands from the mat without having the roll come undone.

10. Get your hands slightly wet and gently pick up the roll. If any ingredients have smashed out of the seam, grab a small amount of sushi rice to cover the exposed ingredients. It's important to have a consistent layer of rice covering the roll; otherwise, the pieces will fall apart when the roll is cut. If you add rice, use the mat to form the rice to the rest of the roll.

11. Once the roll is sealed, place the tempura wakame on top of the roll. Drape the mat over the seaweed and gently press until you feel the tempura forming around the roll. This makes a satisfying crunching sound.

12. Repeat steps 5 through 11 to make three more rolls.

13. Set the mat aside and slice each roll in half. Stack the halves side by side, then slice the halves in half again, and then in half again for a total of 8 pieces per roll.

TIP: When using cream cheese in sushi, it's easier to lay down the cream cheese first and then the rest of the ingredients.

ASPARAGUS ROLL

MAKES 4 SMALL ROLLS OR 24 PIECES ✳ PREP TIME: 15 MINUTES

Asparagus is a low-calorie, nutrient-dense vegetable that makes a great addition to sushi. It's high in fiber, potassium, and folate. Depending on your preferences, you can blanch asparagus for different amounts of time to change its consistency. The longer you boil the asparagus, the softer it gets. Serve this roll with thin slices of lemon to brighten the flavor.

4 half sheets nori
2 cups sushi rice
1 bunch asparagus,
   blanched

1. Place a bamboo mat on the countertop and set a bowl of water beside it.

2. Place a half sheet of nori on the mat, with the smooth side of the nori facedown and the longest edge parallel to the bottom edge of the mat.

3. Dip one hand into the water and rub your hands together. Your hands should be glossy wet, but not dripping. Spread ½ cup of rice across the nori in a layer 2 to 3 grains deep, leaving a ½-inch clear border at the top of the nori.

4. Place one-fourth of the asparagus in a straight line across the center of the rice-covered portion. If your asparagus is less than ½ inch in diameter, feel free to use more than one piece until each bundle is about ½ inch thick.

5. Tuck your thumbs under the mat, hold the asparagus with your fingers, and roll the mat up and over the ingredients until the bottom edge of the seaweed touches the bare rice.

6. Give the roll a firm squeeze to make sure there is no excess air inside the roll. You should be able to slowly remove your hands from the mat without having the roll come undone. If any ingredients are poking out, use your fingertips to tuck them back in.

7. Dip your fingers into the water again and transfer just enough to dampen the bare strip of nori. Continue rolling forward until the damp nori is covered. Give the roll one firm squeeze to seal.

8. Repeat steps 2 through 7 to make three more rolls.

9. Hosomaki is traditionally cut into six pieces. Slice each roll in the middle, stack one half on top of the other, and cut both halves into thirds.

TIP: Try pairing this roll with Vegetarian Miso Mayonnaise, found on page 106.

OSHINKO ROLL

MAKES 4 SMALL ROLLS OR 24 PIECES ✳ PREP TIME: 15 MINUTES

Oshinko translates to "fragrant dish" and refers to Japanese pickled vegetables. Oshinko can be made with various vegetables, but it's most commonly made from pickled daikon radishes. They are vibrantly yellow, pleasantly crunchy, and lightly salty. After opening the package, store any remaining pickled daikon in a sealed container in the refrigerator. Leftover oshinko can be used for chirashi bowls and hand rolls, and as a garnish.

4 half sheets nori
2 cups sushi rice
10 ounces oshinko, cut into matchsticks

1. Place a bamboo mat on the countertop and set a bowl of water beside it.

2. Place a half sheet of nori on the mat, with the smooth side of the nori facedown and the longest edge parallel to the bottom edge of the mat.

3. Dip one hand into the water and rub your hands together. Your hands should be glossy wet, but not dripping. Spread ½ cup of rice across the nori in a layer 2 to 3 grains deep, leaving a ½-inch clear border at the top of the nori.

4. Place one-fourth of the oshinko in a straight line across the center of the rice-covered portion. Use enough to make about a ½-inch-diameter bundle.

5. Tuck your thumbs under the mat, hold the pickled daikon with your fingers, and roll the mat up and over the ingredients until the bottom edge of the nori touches the bare rice.

6. Give the roll a firm squeeze to make sure there is no excess air inside the roll. You should be able to slowly remove your hands from the mat without having the roll come undone. If any ingredients are poking out, use your fingertips to tuck them back in.

7. Dip your fingers into the water again and transfer just enough to dampen the bare strip of nori. Continue rolling forward until the damp nori is covered. Give the roll one firm squeeze to seal.

8. Repeat steps 2 through 7 to make three more rolls.

9. Hosomaki is traditionally cut into six pieces. Slice each roll in the middle, stack one half on top of the other, and cut the halves into thirds.

TIP: Thinly sliced vegetables taste better than thickly sliced ones, due to the greater surface area. Slice your daikon into thin pieces.

SEITAN DRAGON ROLL

MAKES 4 ROLLS OR 32 PIECES ✳ PREP TIME: 30 MINUTES ✳ COOK TIME: 1 HOUR 30 MINUTES

The kind of seitan you use can make or break a recipe. Look for seitan that contains other types of flour, not just vital wheat gluten, because wheat gluten alone makes for incredibly tough and chewy seitan. For a recipe on homemade seitan, please see the References section on page 114. The ideal seitan can be sliced into 1½-inch-by-3-inch slices that are ¼ inch thick. ◷ **CONTAINS EGG**

8 ounces seitan, sliced (page 114)

4 half sheets nori

2 cups sushi rice

8 ounces Tamago (page 111 or store-bought), cut into ½-inch-by-4-inch strips

1 cucumber, sliced

1 avocado, sliced

½ cup Vegan Spicy Mayonnaise (page 108)

Sesame seeds, toasted

1. If you are making your own seitan, prepare it while the sushi rice is cooking.

2. Place a bamboo rolling mat on the countertop and set a bowl of water beside it.

3. Place a half sheet of nori on the mat with the smooth side of the nori facedown and the longest edge parallel to the bottom edge of the mat.

4. Dip one hand into the water and rub your hands together. Your hands should be glossy wet, but not dripping. Spread ½ cup of rice across the entire sheet of nori in a layer 2 to 3 grains deep.

5. Flip the rice and nori mat over so the rice is facedown. Place 2 strips of tamago end to end across the center of the rice and 2 or 3 cucumber slices next to the tamago.

6. Tuck your thumbs under the bamboo mat, hold the ingredients with your fingers, and roll the mat up and over the ingredients until you reach the end of the mat.

7. Give the roll a firm squeeze to make sure there is no excess air inside the roll. You should be able to slowly remove your hands from the mat without having the roll come undone.

8. Get your hands slightly wet and gently pick up the roll. If any ingredients have smashed out of the seam, grab a small amount of sushi rice to cover the exposed ingredients. It's important to have a consistent layer of rice covering the roll; otherwise, the pieces will fall apart when the roll is cut. If you add rice, use the mat to form the rice to the rest of the roll.

9. Place 2 avocado slices on top of the roll, staggering them slightly. Place 1 seitan slice on top of the roll, next to the avocado. Repeat until the entire roll is covered with avocado and seitan. Drape the mat on top of the roll and gently squeeze the mat to form the ingredients to the rice.

10. Repeat steps 2 through 9 to make three more rolls.

11. Slice each roll into 8 even pieces. The ingredients tend to be slippery, so you can use a piece of plastic wrap on top of the rolls to hold everything in place while you cut.

12. Drizzle the vegan spicy mayo on top of the roll and sprinkle with toasted sesame seeds.

TIP: Mix and match this roll! Try different seitan recipes with the different sauce recipes in this book.

MISO-GLAZED SWEET POTATO ROLL

MAKES 4 ROLLS OR 32 PIECES ✳ PREP TIME: 40 MINUTES ✳ COOK TIME: 20 MINUTES

This roll is the perfect blend of sweet and savory—plus, it's filling without being heavy. This recipe will teach you how to add avocado on top of a roll in a very artistic way (it looks more complicated than it really is). The secret to this recipe is basting the sweet potatoes with a miso glaze, plus brushing the top of the roll with soy sauce.

3 tablespoons awase miso paste (see page 3)
1½ tablespoons rice wine vinegar
1 tablespoon maple syrup
2 teaspoons toasted sesame oil
1 sweet potato, peeled and cut into ½-inch-thick matchsticks
4 half sheets nori
2 cups sushi rice
1 cucumber, sliced
1½ avocados, sliced
2 tablespoons soy sauce

1. Preheat the oven to 375°F.

2. In a large bowl, whisk together the miso paste, vinegar, maple syrup, and sesame oil until blended evenly.

3. Put the sweet potato in the marinade and toss until evenly coated. Marinate the potatoes until ready to use.

4. When the oven is preheated, place the sweet potatoes on a baking sheet and bake for 10 minutes. Carefully flip the pieces, brush with marinade, and bake for another 10 minutes. Test them by piercing with a fork. They should be tender but still firm. If too firm, brush with more marinade and bake for 5 more minutes. Once they've reached the desired tenderness, transfer them to a wire rack to cool. Save the remaining marinade.

5. Place a bamboo mat on the countertop and set a bowl of water beside it.

6. Place a half sheet of nori on the mat, with the smooth side of the nori facedown and the longest edge parallel to the bottom edge of the mat.

7. Dip one hand into the water and rub your hands together. Your hands should be glossy wet, but not dripping. Spread ½ cup of rice across the entire sheet of nori in a layer 2 to 3 grains deep.

8. Flip the rice and nori mat over so the rice is facedown. Place 2 or 3 pieces of sweet potato across the center of the nori and lean 2 or 3 pieces of cucumber against them.

9. Tuck your thumbs under the bamboo mat, hold the ingredients with your fingers, and roll the mat up and over the ingredients until you reach the end of the mat.

10. Give the roll a firm squeeze to make sure there is no excess air inside the roll. You should be able to slowly remove your hands from the mat without having the roll come undone.

11. Get your hands slightly wet and gently pick up your roll. If any ingredients have smashed out of the seam, grab a small amount of sushi rice to cover them. It's important to have a consistent layer of rice covering the roll; otherwise, the pieces will fall apart when the roll is cut. If you add rice, use the mat to form the rice to the rest of the roll.

12. Place one avocado half on a cutting board, parallel to the bottom. Starting with the tapered end, slice the avocado as thinly as possible, keeping the cuts perpendicular to the avocado's edge. Repeat with the remaining avocado. The goal is 30 to 40 (⅛-inch-thick) slices.

13. Slowly spread out the avocado slices by using one hand to push the slices to one side and your other hand to help the slices slide across the board. Keep pushing until you can cover the length of the roll (you can use the roll as a guide). Slowly slide a knife underneath the avocado, lift the slices, and transfer to the top of the roll. Drape the bamboo mat on top of the roll and carefully squeeze the mat to form the avocado to the rice.

14. Place a large piece of plastic wrap over the roll.

15. Repeat steps 6 through 14 to make three more rolls. Slice each roll into 8 pieces. Remove the plastic wrap.

16. Stir the soy sauce into the remaining glaze. Brush the rolls with a small amount of glaze and arrange on a plate.

TERIYAKI JACKFRUIT ROLL

MAKES 4 ROLLS OR 32 PIECES ✳ PREP TIME: 30 MINUTES ✳ COOK TIME: 40 MINUTES

Jackfruit is a mildly sweet fruit that can easily take on the consistency of meat. For this recipe, I like to use unripened jackfruit in brine. You don't want to use jackfruit in a syrup because it's far too sweet to be used in sushi.

Olive oil

20-ounce can unripened jackfruit in brine, drained, rinsed, and cored

3 tablespoons teriyaki sauce, divided, plus more for drizzling

¼ cup water

4 half sheets nori

2 cups sushi rice

1 cucumber, sliced

1 avocado, sliced

1 red bell pepper, cut into matchsticks

1 cup cooked spinach

Toasted sesame seeds, for garnish

1. In a skillet over medium heat, heat a splash of olive oil. Once hot, add the jackfruit and cook for 4 to 5 minutes. Mix together 1 tablespoon of teriyaki sauce and the water, then pour the mixture into the pan. Simmer the jackfruit until the water has completely evaporated.

2. Shred the jackfruit using two forks and mix in the remaining 2 tablespoons of teriyaki sauce. Cook the jackfruit for another minute or two before removing it from the pan. Let it cool to room temperature.

3. Place a bamboo mat on the countertop and set a bowl of water beside it.

4. Place a half sheet of nori on the mat, with the smooth side of the nori facedown and the longest edge parallel to the bottom edge of the mat.

5. Dip one hand into the water and rub your hands together. Your hands should be glossy wet, but not dripping. Spread ¼ cup of rice across the entire sheet of nori in a layer 2 to 3 grains deep. Flip the rice and nori mat over so the rice is facedown.

6. Mold ⅛ cup of jackfruit into a line across the center of the nori. Lean 2 or 3 cucumber slices against the jackfruit on the side farthest from you and 2 or 3 avocado slices on the side closest to you. Add 2 or 3 bell pepper strips on top of the cucumber and a thin layer of spinach on the avocado. The ingredient placement is important.

7. Tuck your thumbs under the bamboo mat, hold the ingredients with your fingers, and roll the mat up and over the ingredients until you reach the end of the mat.

8. Give the roll a firm squeeze to make sure there is no excess air inside the roll. You should be able to slowly remove your hands from the mat without having the roll come undone.

9. Get your hands slightly wet and gently pick up the roll. If any ingredients have smashed out of the seam, grab a small amount of sushi rice to cover them. It's important to have a consistent layer of rice covering the roll; otherwise, the pieces will fall apart when the roll is cut. If you add rice, use the mat to form the rice to the rest of the roll.

10. Repeat steps 4 through 9 to make three more rolls.

11. Slice each roll into 8 even pieces and arrange on a plate. Drizzle with teriyaki sauce and sprinkle with sesame seeds.

TIP: Don't squeeze too hard when rolling or you will squeeze water out of the jackfruit!

FRIED SHIITAKE ROLL

MAKES 3 ROLLS OR 36 PIECES ✳ PREP TIME: 35 MINUTES ✳ COOK TIME: 20 MINUTES

Sometimes the soft yet crispy texture of traditional tempura batter is the best option, but other times you want a crunchy, golden-brown layer of breading. This recipe uses a 50/50 mix of cornstarch and flour to maximize the rich color and deep crunch of fried shiitake mushrooms. 🥚 CONTAINS EGG

8 shiitake mushrooms

1 cup boiling water

Peanut oil

2 eggs or the equivalent amount of egg substitute

2 tablespoons water

¼ cup all-purpose flour

¼ cup cornstarch

3 full sheets nori

2 cups sushi rice

½ bunch asparagus, blanched

½ cucumber, sliced

4 scallions, sliced

Vegan Spicy Mayonnaise (page 108)

Nanami togarashi (Japanese seven spice)

1. In a bowl, cover the shiitake mushrooms with the boiling water. Let them soak for at least 10 minutes. Remove the mushrooms from the water and let them cool. Once cool to the touch, slice the mushrooms in half and discard the stems. Squeeze as much water out of the caps as you can.

2. Fill a skillet with at least 2 inches of peanut oil and place over medium-high heat. Line a plate with a few paper towels and rest a pair of tongs on top.

3. In a small bowl, whisk the eggs and water together. In a separate bowl, mix the flour and cornstarch until thoroughly blended.

4. When the oil reaches at least 375°F, or when a sprinkle of cornstarch bubbles immediately, it is ready. Working with one mushroom piece at a time, dip it into the egg mixture, let it drip, toss it in the flour mixture until evenly coated, and then carefully add it to the oil. Repeat until 5 or 6 pieces are in the oil.

5. When the mushrooms turn pale yellow, use the tongs to transfer them to the paper towel–lined plate to drain. They will turn golden brown while resting. Repeat steps 4 and 5 until all the mushrooms are fried.

6. Place a bamboo mat on the countertop and set a bowl of water beside it.

7. Place a sheet of nori on the mat, with the smooth side of the nori facedown and the longest edge parallel to the cotton strings.

8. Dip one hand into the water and rub your hands together. Your hands should be glossy wet, but not dripping. Spread one-third of the rice across the nori in a layer 2 to 3 grains deep, leaving a ½-inch clear border at the top of the nori.

9. Place one-third each of the fried mushrooms, asparagus, cucumber, and scallions across the center of the rice. Make sure that you are using consistent coverage of each of the ingredients.

10. Tuck your thumbs under the mat, hold the ingredients with your fingers, and roll the mat up and over the ingredients until the bottom edge of the nori touches the bare rice.

11. Give the roll a firm squeeze to make sure there is no excess air inside your roll. You should be able to slowly remove your hands from the mat without having the roll come undone. If any ingredients are poking out, use your fingertips to tuck them back in.

12. Dip your fingers into the water again and transfer just enough to dampen the bare strip of nori. Continue rolling forward until the damp nori is pressed against the dry exterior side of the nori.

13. Repeat steps 7 through 12 to make two more rolls.

14. Slice each roll into 12 equal pieces, arrange them on a plate, and drizzle with spicy mayonnaise. For some additional heat, sprinkle with the seven spice as well!

TIP: When frying ingredients that contain a lot of water, such as mushrooms, it's best to use a splash screen over the pan.

GREEN VEGAN ROLL

MAKES 4 ROLLS OR 32 PIECES ✳ PREP TIME: 30 MINUTES ✳ COOK TIME: 15 MINUTES

This recipe has it all: It's crunchy, savory, spicy, and very satisfying. The *furikake* (rice sprinkles) add a unique flavor as well as an extra pop of color. This bright and nutritious sushi roll is sure to become a staple in your vegan sushi lineup. The roll pairs well with Vegan Spicy Mayonnaise (page 108), Garlic Mayonnaise (page 107), Vegetarian Miso Mayonnaise (page 106), or eel sauce.

8 shiitake mushrooms
1 cup boiling water
4 half sheets nori
2 cups sushi rice
2 ounces furikake
1 carrot, sliced
1 avocado, sliced
½ cucumber, sliced
4 ounces kimchi

1. In a bowl, cover the shiitake mushrooms with the boiling water. Let them soak for at least 10 minutes. Remove the mushrooms from the water and let them cool. Once cool to the touch, slice them in half and discard the stems. Squeeze as much water out of the caps as you can.

2. Place a bamboo mat on the countertop and set a bowl of water beside it.

3. Place a half-sheet of nori on the mat, with the smooth side of the nori facedown and the longest edge parallel to the bottom edge of the mat.

4. Dip one hand into the water and rub your hands together. Your hands should be glossy wet, but not dripping. Spread ½ cup of rice across the entire sheet of nori in a layer 2 to 3 grains deep. Sprinkle an even layer of furikake on top of the rice.

5. Flip the rice and nori mat over so the rice is facedown. Place 2 or 3 carrot slices, avocado slices, and cucumber slices across the center of the nori. Place 3 or 4 mushroom pieces on top of the other ingredients, then a thin layer of kimchi. Make sure that you are using consistent coverage of each of the ingredients.

6. Tuck your thumbs under the bamboo mat, hold the ingredients with your fingers, and roll the mat up and over the ingredients until you reach the end of the mat.

7. Give the roll a firm squeeze to make sure there is no excess air inside the roll. You should be able to slowly remove your hands from the mat without having the roll come undone.

8. Get your hands slightly wet and gently pick up the roll. If any ingredients have smashed out of the seam, grab a small amount of rice to cover them. It's important to have a consistent layer of rice covering the roll; otherwise, the pieces will fall apart when the roll is cut. If you add rice, use the mat to form the rice to the rest of the roll.

9. Repeat steps 3 through 8 to make three more rolls.

10. Slice each roll into 8 even pieces and arrange on a plate.

TIP: If you want to reduce the number of crunchy ingredients, you can blanch or roast the carrots.

SPICY MANGO ROLL

MAKES 4 ROLLS OR 32 PIECES ✳ PREP TIME: 30 MINUTES ✳ COOK TIME: 15 MINUTES

It's hard to find something that is both spicy and refreshing, but this recipe hits the spot. Crisp jalapeños and dots of sriracha provide plenty of heat, while the cucumber, cream cheese, and mango add a contrasting coolness. Crunchy wonton strips blend the flavors together to create a crowd-pleasing dish. If you find this roll too spicy, you can replace the sriracha with Vegan Spicy Mayonnaise (page 108). 🥚 **CONTAINS EGG**

Peanut oil
⅛ **pack wonton wrappers**
4 half sheets nori
2 cups sushi rice
Toasted black
  sesame seeds
4 ounces cream cheese
1 mango, sliced
2 jalapeños, seeded and
  cut into matchsticks
½ cucumber, sliced
2 ounces sriracha
4 scallions, sliced

1. Fill a skillet with 1 inch of peanut oil and put it over high heat. Line a plate with paper towels.

2. Take a stack of 4 or 5 wonton wrappers and fold them in half. Slice them as thinly as possible into strips and then rub them between your fingers to separate the strips.

3. Once the oil reaches 375°F, gently add a small handful of wonton strips. Ideally, you would spread out the strips so they don't clump together as they fry, but sometimes it can't be helped. When the strips turn a nice golden brown, use a pair of tongs to transfer them to the paper towel–lined plate.

4. Place a bamboo mat on the countertop and set a bowl of water beside it.

5. Place a half sheet of nori on the mat, with the smooth side of the nori facedown and the longest edge parallel to the bottom edge of the mat.

6. Dip one hand into the water and rub your hands together. Your hands should be glossy wet, but not dripping. Spread ½ cup of rice across the entire sheet of nori in a layer 2 to 3 grains deep. Sprinkle the sesame seeds over the rice.

7. Flip the rice and nori mat over so the rice is facedown and gently press down on the nori to get the seeds to stick to the rice. Take one-fourth of the cream cheese and use your finger and thumb to pinch/press the cream cheese onto the center of the nori, moving from one side to the other.

8. Place 2 or 3 mango strips against the cream cheese on the side closest to you. Place 2 or 3 jalapeño and cucumber slices on the side of the cream cheese farthest from you. Spread a small handful of fried wonton strips on top of the ingredients. Feel free to break up the wonton strips if they are too wide or long to fit inside the roll.

9. Tuck your thumbs under the bamboo mat, hold the ingredients with your fingers, and roll the mat up and over the ingredients until you reach the end of the mat.

10. Give the roll a firm squeeze to make sure there is no excess air inside the roll. You should be able to slowly remove your hands from the mat without having the roll come undone.

11. Get your hands slightly wet and gently pick up the roll. If any ingredients have smashed out of the seam, grab a small amount of sushi rice to cover them. It's important to have a consistent layer of rice covering the roll; otherwise, the pieces will fall apart when the roll is cut. If you add rice, use the mat to form the rice to the rest of the roll.

12. Repeat steps 5 through 11 to make three more rolls.

13. Slice each roll into 8 even pieces and arrange them on a plate. Squeeze a small dot of sriracha onto each piece and sprinkle with the sliced scallions.

TIP: I prefer to fry several wonton wrappers at one time and store them in a covered container until I want to use them. They are great for adding extra crunch to any dish.

MISO-GLAZED SEITAN SHIITAKE ROLL

MAKES 3 ROLLS OR 36 PIECES ✳ PREP TIME: 30 MINUTES ✳ COOK TIME: 30 MINUTES

Seitan and miso pair wonderfully together in this roll. The fresh vegetables mixed with savory seitan create a well-balanced, nutrient-dense dish. I always make more of these rolls than I expect people to eat, because they go fast. If you plan on bringing this dish to a party, add the spicy mayo just before serving.

6 to 8 shiitake mushrooms

1 cup boiling water

1 tablespoon awase miso paste (see page 3)

1 tablespoon warm water

2 tablespoons mirin

2 tablespoons soy sauce, plus 1 teaspoon, divided

1 teaspoon brown sugar

4 ounces seitan strips

2 tablespoons vegetable oil, divided

1 garlic clove, minced

1 teaspoon grated fresh ginger

3 full sheets nori

2 cups sushi rice

½ cucumber, cut into matchsticks

½ avocado, sliced

1 carrot, cut into matchsticks

½ red bell pepper, cut into matchsticks

Vegan Spicy Mayonnaise (page 108)

2 scallions, sliced

1. In a small bowl, cover the mushrooms with the boiling water. Let them soak for at least 10 minutes. Remove the mushrooms from the water and let them cool. Once cool to the touch, slice them in half and discard the stems. Squeeze as much water out of the caps as possible.

2. In a separate small bowl, mix the miso paste, warm water, mirin, 1 teaspoon of soy sauce, and the brown sugar together. Add the seitan and let it soak for at least 10 minutes.

3. In a skillet, heat 1 tablespoon of oil over medium-high heat. Brown the seitan on both sides and then reduce the heat to low. Add the remaining marinade to the pan and cook until the liquid is absorbed, about 10 minutes. Flip the seitan at least once.

4. In a separate skillet, heat the remaining 1 tablespoon of oil over high heat. Add the mushrooms and cook for 2 to 3 minutes, until the caps start to shrivel. Add the remaining 2 tablespoons of soy sauce, the garlic, and the ginger, and cook for another 2 minutes.

5. Place a bamboo mat on the countertop and set a bowl of water beside it.

6. Place a sheet of nori on the mat, with the smooth side of the nori facedown and the longest edge parallel to the cotton strings.

7. Dip one hand into the water and rub your hands together. Your hands should be glossy wet, but not dripping. Spread one-third of the rice across the nori in a layer 2 to 3 grains deep, leaving a ½-inch clear border at the top of the nori.

8. Place one-third of the seitan, mushrooms, cucumber, avocado, carrot, and bell pepper across the center of the rice. The total diameter of the ingredients should not exceed 1 inch. Make sure that you are using consistent coverage of each of the ingredients (generally 2 or 3 pieces of each ingredient).

9. Tuck your thumbs under the mat, hold the ingredients with your fingers, and roll the mat up and over the ingredients until the bottom edge of the nori touches the bare rice.

10. Give the roll a firm squeeze to make sure there's no excess air inside the roll. You should be able to slowly remove your hands from the mat without having the roll come undone. If any ingredients are poking out, use your fingertips to tuck them back in.

11. Dip your fingers into the water again and transfer just enough to dampen the bare strip of nori. Continue rolling forward until the damp nori is pressed against the dry exterior side of the nori.

12. Repeat steps 6 through 11 to make two more rolls.

13. Slice each roll into 12 equal pieces and arrange on a plate. Drizzle with spicy mayonnaise and sprinkle with the scallions.

TIP: Raw vegetables work well in this recipe, but you could easily modify the taste by preparing the same vegetables in different ways; for example, blanching the carrots, pickling the cucumbers, or grilling the bell peppers.

FRUITY DESSERT ROLL

MAKES 4 ROLLS OR 32 PIECES ✳ PREP TIME: 25 MINUTES

Dessert sushi can be a real hit or a total flop, but this recipe is a home run! Sushi rice may not seem like an ideal ingredient for a dessert, but it can be surprisingly good, and it helps keep this dessert from becoming too sweet. Soy paper, which is thin and with minimal flavor, is a natural choice for this roll, but you need to be extra careful not to get it wet, or it will quickly become unusable.

3 sheets soy paper
Coconut oil
2 cups sushi rice
**4 ounces chocolate-
   hazelnut spread**
2 bananas, sliced
4 to 8 strawberries, sliced
Whipped cream
Ground cinnamon
2 ounces raisins

1. Gently fold 3 sheets of soy paper down the middle to create a crease. Then, cut them in half, using the crease as a guide. Carefully stack them and set them aside. Place one piece on a rolling mat with the longest side parallel to the bottom of the mat.

2. Rub a small amount of coconut oil on your hands. This will help prevent the soy paper from accidentally getting soggy. Spread ½ cup of rice across the entire piece of soy paper in a layer 3 to 4 grains deep.

3. Carefully flip the soy paper over so that the rice is touching the rolling mat. Use a butter knife to spread a generous layer of chocolate-hazelnut spread in a line across the center of the soy paper. Place 2 banana slices and 4 to 8 strawberry slices in a straight line on top of the spread.

4. Tuck your thumbs under the bamboo mat, hold the ingredients with your fingers, and roll the mat up and over the ingredients until the bottom edge of the rice touches the soy paper.

5. Give the roll a gentle squeeze to make sure there is no excess air inside the roll. You should be able to slowly remove your hands from the mat without

having the roll come undone. If any ingredients are poking out, use your fingertips to tuck them back in.

6. Continue rolling forward until you reach the end of the mat. If any ingredients have smashed out of the seam, grab a small amount of sushi rice to cover them. It's important to have a consistent layer of rice covering the roll; otherwise, the pieces will fall apart when the roll is cut. If you add rice, use the mat to form the rice to the rest of the roll.

7. Repeat steps 2 through 6 to make three more rolls.

8. Slice each roll into 8 even pieces, making sure to wipe your knife between each cut. Lay the pieces on their sides in two even rows on plates. Spray a small mound of whipped cream on top of each piece, dust with cinnamon, and sprinkle with the raisins.

TIP: This recipe can be made vegan by using coconut whipped cream and making your own chocolate-hazelnut spread.

VEGAN "SCALLOP" ROLL

MAKES 6 ROLLS OR 36 PIECES ✳ PREP TIME: 5 MINUTES ✳ COOK TIME: 30 MINUTES

King oyster mushrooms have a meatier texture than most mushrooms and work wonderfully as a scallop substitute. These mushrooms can absorb flavors like a sponge! It's best to avoid getting mushrooms wet before putting them in hot oil, so if there is visible dirt, brush them lightly with a paper towel. The *kaiware* (sprouted daikon radish sprouts) add a nice peppery flavor and bring more color to the roll.

Peanut oil
1 cup egg substitute
2 tablespoons water
¼ cup all-purpose flour
¼ cup cornstarch
2 ounces king oyster
  mushrooms, capped and
  quartered lengthwise
6 half sheets nori
2 cups sushi rice
1 ounce daikon radish
  sprouts (kaiware)
Garlic Mayonnaise
  (page 107)

1. Fill a skillet with at least 2 inches of peanut oil and place over medium-high heat. Line a plate with paper towels and rest a pair of tongs on top.

2. In a small bowl, whisk the egg substitute. In a separate bowl, mix the flour and cornstarch until thoroughly blended.

3. When the oil reaches at least 375°F, or when a sprinkle of cornstarch bubbles immediately, it is ready. Working with one mushroom piece at a time, dip it into the egg mixture, let it drip, toss it in the flour mixture until evenly coated, and then carefully add it to the oil. Repeat until 5 or 6 pieces are in the oil.

4. When the mushrooms turn pale yellow, use the tongs to transfer them to the paper towel–lined plate to drain. They will turn golden brown while resting. Repeat steps 3 and 4 until all the mushrooms are fried.

5. Place a bamboo mat on the countertop and set a bowl of water beside it.

6. Place a half sheet of nori on the mat, with the smooth side of the nori facedown and the longest edge parallel to the cotton strings.

7. Dip one hand into the water and rub your hands together. Your hands should be glossy wet, but not dripping. Spread one-third of the rice across the nori in a layer 2 to 3 grains deep, leaving a ½-inch clear border at the top of the nori.

8. Place 1 or 2 pieces of fried mushroom across the center of the rice. Cut a 1-inch-diameter bundle of radish sprouts off their seeds and place an equal amount on either side of the mushrooms.

9. Tuck your thumbs under the bamboo mat, hold the ingredients with your fingers, and roll the mat up and over the ingredients until the bottom edge of the nori touches the bare rice.

10. Give the roll a firm squeeze to make sure there is no excess air inside the roll. You should be able to slowly remove your hands from the mat without having the roll come undone. If any ingredients are poking out, use your fingertips to tuck them back in.

11. Dip your fingers into the water again and transfer just enough to dampen the bare strip of nori. Continue rolling forward until the damp nori is pressed against the dry exterior side of the nori.

12. Repeat steps 6 through 11 to make five more rolls.

13. Slice each roll into 6 equal pieces, arrange on plates, and drizzle with garlic mayonnaise.

TIP: Once you get comfortable rolling this recipe, you can make two rolls at a time by placing two half sheets side by side on your mat.

RED BELL ROLL

MAKES 4 ROLLS OR 24 PIECES ✳ PREP TIME: 30 MINUTES

This roll is quick to make, lightly sweet, and very colorful. Inari and mango blend smoothly with the avocado. The scallion and red bell pepper keep this roll crisp and refreshing. This roll is fun to make because it's in the futomaki style, but with the rice on the outside.

4 half sheets nori

2 cups sushi rice

**Toasted black
    sesame seeds**

½ red bell pepper, sliced

1 avocado, sliced

**2 inari pouches, cut into
    ⅛-inch strips**

1 mango, sliced

**4 scallions, green
    parts only, cut into
    4-inch pieces**

1. Place a bamboo mat on the countertop and set a bowl of water beside it.

2. Place a half sheet of nori on the mat, with the smooth side of the nori facedown and the longest edge parallel to the cotton strings.

3. Dip one hand into the water and rub your hands together. Your hands should be glossy wet, but not dripping. Spread ½ cup of rice across the nori in a layer 2 to 3 grains deep, leaving a ½-inch clear border at the top of the nori. Sprinkle sesame seeds evenly over the rice.

4. Gently flip the nori over so that the rice is on the bottom and the uncovered portion of the nori is now closest to you. Place 2 or 3 pieces of bell pepper, avocado, and inari, plus 1 mango slice and 1 piece of scallion, in a straight line across the center of the nori.

5. Tuck your thumbs under the bamboo mat, hold the ingredients with your fingers, and roll the mat up and over the ingredients until the bottom edge of the nori touches the bare rice.

6. Give the roll a firm squeeze to make sure there is no excess air in the roll. You should be able to slowly remove your hands from the mat without having the roll come undone. If any ingredients are poking out from underneath the seam, continue rolling until you reach the end of the mat.

7. Repeat steps 2 through 6 to make three more rolls.

8. Slice each roll into 6 equal pieces (this will be harder than normal), making sure to wipe your knife between each slice. Transfer your pieces to plates and enjoy!

TIP: If you don't mind the taste of seaweed on the outside of the roll, this roll works really well in the futomaki style.

SAKURA HAND ROLL

MAKES 6 HAND ROLLS ✳ PREP TIME: 25 MINUTES ✳ COOK TIME: 15 MINUTES

Hand rolls are a fun and fast way to serve sushi at a party because they don't need chopsticks or plates. This recipe features sushi rice that has been dyed pink with beet juice for extra flavor and aesthetic appeal.

2 cups sushi rice
Unsweetened beet juice
6 half sheets nori
1 avocado, sliced
1 cucumber, sliced
1 large carrot, sliced
6 to 10 asparagus stalks,
    blanched
Sesame seeds

TIP: If you're having difficulty with temaki, try making the kite pattern with the rice in a different corner of the nori.

1. After the sushi rice has been seasoned but before it has cooled, sprinkle it with 1 tablespoon of beet juice at a time, making sure to fold it into the rice as you sprinkle, until the rice reaches your desired shade of pink.

2. Place a bamboo mat on the countertop and set a bowl of water beside it. Place a half sheet of nori on the mat, with the smooth side of the nori facedown and the longest edge parallel to the cotton strings.

3. Dip one hand into the water and rub your hands together. Your hands should be glossy wet, but not dripping. Put ⅓ cup of rice on the nori and slowly spread it out to create the shape of a kite. The layer of rice should be 2 to 3 grains thick.

4. Place one-sixth of the avocado, cucumber, carrot, and asparagus along the centerline of the kite. If you find that you are running out of space at the bottom, you can fan the fillings out toward the top of the kite.

5. Gently slide the roll into your nondominant hand, keeping the top of the kite pointing away from you. Wrap the nori around the kite and use a few grains of rice as rice paste to seal the fillings inside. The finished roll should look something like an ice-cream cone.

6. Repeat steps 2 through 5 to make five more hand rolls.

AVOCADO MANGO HAND ROLL

MAKES 6 HAND ROLLS ✳ PREP TIME: 25 MINUTES

Hand rolls are meant to be fast, so they typically aren't meant to be filling on their own. Generally speaking, someone should be able to enjoy three or four hand rolls before feeling satiated. That's why it's important to create variety in your hand rolls.

6 half sheets nori
2 cups sushi rice
1 avocado, sliced
1 red bell pepper, sliced
1 mango, sliced
½ cucumber, sliced
1 bunch radish sprouts

TIP: Since hand rolls aren't meant to be very filling, don't feel obligated to pack them with lots of ingredients.

1. Place a bamboo mat on the countertop and set a bowl of water beside it.

2. Place a half sheet of nori on the mat, with the smooth side of the nori facedown and the longest edge parallel to the cotton strings.

3. Dip one hand into the water and rub your hands together. Your hands should be glossy wet, but not dripping. Put ⅓ cup of rice on the nori and slowly spread it out to create the shape of a kite. The layer of rice should be 2 to 3 grains thick.

4. Fan out 4 or 5 avocado slices along the top portion of the kite. Place 3 or 4 bell pepper slices on top of the avocado.

5. Place 4 or 5 thin mango slices between the bell pepper. Place one-sixth of the cucumber pieces on top of the mango. If you find that you are running out of space at the bottom, you can fan the fillings out toward the top of the kite. Fan out a small number of sprouts, equivalent to about ¼ inch in diameter per hand roll.

6. Gently slide the roll into your nondominant hand, keeping the top of the kite pointing away from you. Wrap the nori around the kite and use a few grains of rice as rice paste to seal the fillings inside.

SPICY JACKFRUIT HAND ROLL

MAKES 6 HAND ROLLS ✳ PREP TIME: 30 MINUTES

Many recipes usually call for processed jackfruit (whether canned in brine, syrup, or cooked), but in this recipe I wanted to highlight the flavor and texture of raw jackfruit. Using raw jackfruit may seem intimidating at first, but I promise you it is worth trying and definitely worth the work! I recommend wearing gloves and covering the cutting surface with a paper bag for easy cleanup, as jackfruit naturally releases a latex-like residue when sliced. **CONTAINS EGG**

¼ raw jackfruit
6 half sheets nori
2 cups sushi rice
1 avocado, sliced
2 jalapeños, seeded and cut into matchsticks
Garlic Mayonnaise (page 107)
1 tablespoon olive oil

1. Wearing a pair of disposable gloves, remove the seed pods from the jackfruit. The bright yellow/orange fruit around the hard seeds is what we want to keep. Remove the thin membrane around each seed. Discard the seeds and any white "tendons." Slice the bottoms off the fruit and split them in half. Slice each half into 3 strips.
2. Place a bamboo mat on the countertop and set a bowl of water beside it.
3. Place a half sheet of nori on the mat, with the smooth side of the nori facedown and the longest edge parallel to the cotton strings.
4. Dip one hand into the water and rub your hands together. Your hands should be glossy wet, but not dripping. Put ⅓ cup of rice on the nori and slowly spread it out to create the shape of a kite. The layer of rice should be 2 to 3 grains thick.
5. Fan out 4 or 5 avocado slices along the top portion of the kite. Place 3 or 4 jalapeño strips on top of the avocado. Place 5 or 6 jackfruit slices on top of the other ingredients.

CONTINUED

SPICY JACKFRUIT HAND ROLL (CONTINUED)

6. If you find that you are running out of space at the bottom, you can push some of the jackfruit toward the top of the kite.

7. Gently slide the roll into your nondominant hand, keeping the top of the kite pointing away from you. Wrap the nori around the kite and use a few grains of rice as rice paste to seal the fillings inside. The finished roll should look something like an ice-cream cone.

8. After rolling, feel free to add a few more jackfruit slices. It's always best to make smaller hand rolls, but ingredients shift around so much during the rolling process that it's hard to tell if you have used enough.

9. Repeat steps 2 through 8 to make five more hand rolls.

TIP: You can arrange hand rolls on any plate, but if you find that you enjoy making hand rolls more often than other types of maki, you can buy stands specifically for serving hand rolls online.

TOFU "BACON" BREAKFAST TEMAKI

MAKES 6 HAND ROLLS ✳ PREP TIME: 3 HOURS 30 MINUTES ✳ COOK TIME: 50 MINUTES

Everyone knows about breakfast burritos, but have you ever heard of breakfast sushi? This recipe features smoky tofu "bacon," savory tamago, and buttery, oven-roasted sweet potato wrapped in a hand roll. You can add spice using Vegan Spicy Mayonnaise (page 108) or eat the hand rolls dry. Either way, you're bound to eat more than just one. ⌓ **CONTAINS EGG**

16 ounces extra-firm tofu
½ cup reduced-sodium soy sauce
2 tablespoons tomato paste
2 tablespoons maple syrup
2 tablespoons liquid smoke
2 cups sushi rice
8 ounces Tamago (page 111 or store-bought)
1 sweet potato
3 tablespoons salted butter
1 tablespoon brown sugar
Olive oil cooking spray
6 half sheets nori
Vegan Spicy Mayonnaise (page 108) (optional)

1. Drain the tofu and wrap it in paper towels or a clean cloth. Place it on a baking sheet and set another baking sheet on top. Set a heavy object on top to press out the excess moisture. Let the tofu press for at least 1 hour, but preferably 2 hours.

2. In a medium bowl, whisk together the soy sauce, tomato paste, maple syrup, and liquid smoke. Slice the pressed tofu into ⅛-inch-thick matchsticks and add to the marinade. Marinate for 1 hour in the refrigerator.

3. Preheat the oven to 375°F.

4. Prepare the sushi rice and slice the tamago into large matchsticks.

5. Peel the sweet potato and slice into large matchsticks about ½ inch thick.

6. In a small saucepan over medium heat, melt the butter and stir in the brown sugar. Brush the butter mixture onto the sweet potato matchsticks until evenly coated.

CONTINUED

7. Spread the sweet potatoes on a baking sheet and bake for 10 minutes. Carefully flip them and bake for another 10 minutes. Test them by piercing 1 or 2 with a fork. They should be tender, but still firm. If too firm, bake for an additional 5 minutes. Once they've reached your desired tenderness, transfer them to a wire rack to cool.

8. Spray a baking sheet with cooking spray. Place the tofu sticks on the baking sheet and bake for 20 minutes. Spray the tops of the tofu with cooking spray and gently flip them. Baste the tofu sticks with the marinade and return them to the oven for 15 minutes. Check every 5 minutes, being careful not to burn them.

9. Place a bamboo mat on the countertop and set a bowl of water beside it.

10. Place a half sheet of nori on the mat, with the smooth side of the nori facedown and the longest edge parallel to the cotton strings.

11. Dip one hand into the water and rub your hands together. Your hands should be glossy wet, but not dripping. Put ⅓ cup of rice on the nori and slowly spread it out to create the shape of a kite. The layer of rice should be 2 to 3 grains thick.

12. Fan out 4 or 5 tofu bacon pieces along the top portion of the kite. Place 3 or 4 tamago slices and 3 or 4 sweet potato slices on top.

13. Gently slide the roll into your nondominant hand, keeping the top of the kite pointing away from you. Wrap the nori around the kite and use a few grains of rice as rice paste to seal the fillings inside. The finished roll should look something like an ice-cream cone.

14. Repeat steps 10 through 14 to make five more hand rolls.

15. Drizzle the temaki with spicy mayonnaise, if using, and serve.

TIP: If you have enough space in your oven, cook the sweet potatoes and the tofu at the same time.

Sashimi, Chirashi, Nigiri, Inari, and Other Sushi

VEGAN TOBIKO GUNKAN MAKI

MAKES 6 TO 8 PIECES ✳ PREP TIME: 20 MINUTES ✳ COOK TIME: 20 MINUTES

Vegan tobiko makes a great addition to the wide range of sushi recipes, but this recipe should be reserved for use on top of a roll or as gunkan maki, as it tends to have more liquid than traditional tobiko. The amaranth seeds should be left in the beet juice when stored, and it should be drained just before putting it on top of the sushi.

**2 cups unsweetened
  beet juice**
½ cup amaranth seeds
1 teaspoon smoked paprika
Salt
1 cup sushi rice
**2 or 3 half sheets nori,
  cut lengthwise into
  3 equal strips**
1 bunch scallions, sliced

1. In a small pot, bring the beet juice to a boil. Add the amaranth seeds and stir thoroughly. Boil for 20 minutes, stirring occasionally.

2. Remove from the heat, add the paprika and salt, and pour into a glass container to cool. Once cool, refrigerate the amaranth for at least 20 minutes (ideally overnight).

3. When you are ready to make the gunkan maki, spoon the desired amount of amaranth seeds into a sieve over a bowl and allow to drain. Return the drained beet juice to the original container.

4. Set a bowl of water on the counter.

5. Take a small ball of rice and lightly compress it in one hand, until all the rice can be hidden within your grip. If this can't be done easily, use slightly less rice.

CONTINUED

6. Dip one tip of a nori strip into the water and wrap the nori around the rice ball until the damp portion of the nori sticks to a dry section. There should be enough space to accommodate the vegan tobiko.

7. Use a spoon to add a small amount of vegan tobiko to the top of the gunkan maki. Garnish with a few sliced scallions.

8. Repeat steps 5 through 7 to make the remaining gunkan maki. Arrange the pieces on a plate at a slight angle to serve.

TIP: Use kitchen scissors to cut the nori to your desired width. The wider the strips, the bigger the gunkan maki.

SEAWEED SALAD GUNKAN MAKI

MAKES 6 TO 8 PIECES ✳ PREP TIME: 20 MINUTES

Wakame (seaweed salad) has a unique texture; some would say it's slimy, but I think that's a stretch. Although I don't personally enjoy eating it by itself, I find it enjoyable as gunkan maki topped with fresh tomato and cucumber. Wakame is rich in antioxidants, B vitamins, iodine, and calcium, so this recipe makes healthy bites of vegan bliss.

8 ounces wakame (seaweed salad)

2 ounces ponzu sauce

1 cup sushi rice

2 or 3 half sheets nori, cut lengthwise into 3 equal strips

¼ English or Japanese cucumber, cut into half moons

4 cherry tomatoes, halved

Sesame seeds, toasted, for garnish (optional)

1. In a small bowl, combine the wakame and ponzu until thoroughly mixed.

2. Set a bowl of water on the counter.

3. Grab a small ball of rice and lightly compress it in one hand, until all the rice can be hidden within your grip. If this can't be done easily, use slightly less rice.

4. Dip one tip of a nori strip into the water and wrap it around the rice ball until the damp portion of the nori sticks to a dry section. Use a fork to pick up a small portion of wakame. Twist the fork to wrap the wakame around the fork (like twisting spaghetti). Place the wakame inside the gunkan maki.

5. Slide 3 or 4 cucumber slices into the gunkan maki and place a piece of tomato on top. If using, sprinkle some toasted sesame seeds over the gunkan maki.

6. Repeat steps 3 through 5 to make the remaining gunkan maki.

TIP: This recipe is a great way to use leftover wakame from Dagobah Rolls (page 30).

TAMAGO NIGIRI

MAKES 6 TO 8 PIECES ✳ PREP TIME: 20 MINUTES

Tamago nigiri is a classic form of sushi found worldwide. This iconic piece of nigiri has a thin seaweed "belt" that helps hold the tamago to the ball of rice. There are hundreds of variations of tamago recipes, any of which will work. To make your own tamago, see the recipe on page 111. ⊖ CONTAINS EGG

1 cup sushi rice

6 ounces Tamago (page 111 or store-bought), cut into 6 to 8 (¼-inch-wide) pieces

1 sheet nori, cut into ¼-inch-wide strips

1. Set a bowl of water on the counter.

2. Grab a small ball of rice and lightly compress it in one hand, until all the rice can be hidden within your grip. If this can't be done easily, use slightly less rice. Repeat this step until you have 6 to 8 rice balls.

3. Place a piece of tamago on each rice ball. Dip one end of the nori strip into the water and then wrap the strip around the tamago and rice ball. Continue wrapping it in a straight line until the damp part of the nori touches a dry section. Hold the damp nori in place for a few seconds as it dries.

4. Gently place the piece of nigiri on a plate and repeat step 3 to make the remaining nigiri.

TIP: Cut nori to your desired width by placing the knife edge on the nori and using your nondominant hand to press down on the back of the knife. You can use scissors, but I find that more difficult. Longer strips of seaweed make wrapping the nigiri more difficult, not less.

MUSHROOM NIGIRI

MAKES 6 TO 8 PIECES ✳ PREP TIME: 20 MINUTES ✳ COOK TIME: 20 MINUTES

King oyster mushrooms are perfect for making mushroom nigiri because they are large and meaty and absorb any flavor you cook them with. This easy and mess-free recipe makes a great appetizer for parties.

2 tablespoons unsalted butter, melted

1 tablespoon soy sauce

1 teaspoon honey

1 garlic clove, grated

2 tablespoons sesame oil, divided

4 to 6 ounces king oyster mushrooms, cut into 6 to 8 (¼-inch) slices

1 cup sushi rice

1 sheet nori, cut into ¼-inch-wide strips

Freshly ground black pepper

TIP: King oyster mushrooms go great on chirashi bowls, salads, and in oshizushi.

1. In a bowl, combine the butter, soy sauce, honey, and garlic and stir until blended.

2. In a nonstick skillet over medium-high heat, heat 1 tablespoon of oil. Working in batches if necessary, arrange the mushrooms in the pan so they don't touch. Brush the remaining 1 tablespoon of oil over the mushrooms as they cook. Panfry for 5 minutes on each side.

3. Add the butter sauce and remove the pan from the heat. Toss the mushroom pieces in the sauce until evenly coated. Let them sit in the pan for at least 5 minutes to absorb the sauce.

4. Set a bowl of water on the counter.

5. Grab a small ball of rice and lightly compress it in one hand, until all the rice can be hidden within your grip. If this can't be done easily, use slightly less rice. Repeat this step until you have 6 to 8 rice balls.

6. Place a piece of king oyster mushroom on each rice ball. Dip one end of the nori strip into the water and then wrap the strip around the mushroom and rice ball. Continue wrapping it in a straight line until the damp part of the nori touches a dry section. Hold the damp nori in place for a few seconds as it dries.

7. Gently place the piece of nigiri on a plate and repeat steps 5 and 6 to make the remaining nigiri.

SAKURA INARI

MAKES 6 PIECES ✳ PREP TIME: 35 MINUTES

Inari is a pouch made from fried tofu that usually comes packaged in a sweet sauce. Inari are not meant to be finished in one bite like other types of nigiri. Instead, they can be consumed in multiple bites, which allows us to stuff more ingredients inside each pouch.

1 cup sushi rice
Unsweetened beet juice
Furikake
1 avocado
6 inari pouches
¼ fresh pineapple

TIP: You can tell when a pineapple is ripe by smelling the bottom of the pineapple. If there is very little scent, the pineapple isn't ripe enough.

1. After the sushi rice has been seasoned but before it has cooled, sprinkle it with 1 tablespoon of beet juice at a time, making sure to fold the juice into the rice as you sprinkle, until the rice reaches your desired shade of pink. Once the rice is cool enough to handle, sprinkle it with the furikake and gently mix.

2. Peel and pit the avocado, then slice it into thin strips. Carefully open each inari pouch and tuck 5 to 7 slices of avocado inside. I prefer to have the points of each slice peeking out from the pouch, but you can hide them under the rice if you prefer.

3. Set a bowl of water on the counter. Grab a small ball of rice and lightly compress it in one hand, until all the rice can be hidden within your grip. If this can't be done easily, use slightly less rice. Repeat this step until you have 6 rice balls. Place one rice ball inside each inari pouch.

4. Slice the pineapple into small chunks.

5. Add 3 chunks to each inari pouch and arrange them so that each bite will contain one chunk.

INARI DELUXE

MAKES 6 PIECES ✳ PREP TIME: 30 MINUTES

This recipe focuses on the savory side of inari. Buttery mushrooms, crunchy vegetables, and tangy sushi rice make this dish a well-rounded treat for any occasion. Inari deluxe travels well but should be consumed warm for the best experience. If you're making this recipe for children, you may want to swap out the jalapeño for another crunchy ingredient, such as carrots.

6 inari pouches
2 tablespoons unsalted butter, melted
1 tablespoon soy sauce
1 teaspoon honey
1 garlic clove, peeled and grated
1 tablespoon sesame oil
6 portabella mushrooms, diced small
1 cup sushi rice
1 avocado, peeled, pitted, and diced small
½ red bell pepper, diced small
2 scallions, diced small
1 jalapeño, seeded and diced small

1. Carefully open each inari pouch and set aside.

2. In a small bowl, combine the butter, soy sauce, honey, and garlic and stir until blended.

3. In a nonstick skillet over medium-high heat, heat the oil. Add the mushrooms and slowly stir until the mushrooms have browned on all sides. Pour in the butter mixture and remove the pan from the heat. Stir occasionally until the mushrooms have absorbed most of the sauce.

4. In a large bowl, combine the rice, mushrooms, avocado, red bell pepper, scallions, and jalapeño. Use a rice paddle to stir until evenly distributed. Grab a small handful of the rice mixture and stuff it into an inari pouch. Continue to fill the pouches until they contain the amount desired.

5. Place the inari pouches on a plate, leaning one against another, in a straight line.

TIP: Don't be afraid to substitute or experiment with this recipe. I like to add Vegetarian Miso Mayonnaise (page 106) for an extra umami boost.

TEMPURA TOFU BOWL

MAKES 4 POKE BOWLS ✳ PREP TIME: 1 HOUR ✳ COOK TIME: 1 HOUR

Meat substitutes have come a long way and egg substitutes have as well. This recipe puts egg substitutes to the test with a variety of different tempura-fried vegetables and tempura tofu. Make sure to dry the ingredients thoroughly before deep-frying.

14 ounces firm tofu

1 cup boiling water

8 to 12 shiitake mushroom caps

½ cup soy sauce

¾ cup mirin

4 tablespoons sugar

Peanut oil

6 ounces egg substitute (such as JUST Egg)

½ cup all-purpose flour, sifted

½ cup cornstarch, plus 4 tablespoons, divided

½ bunch asparagus, blanched and dried

Daikon, peeled and shredded into thin matchsticks

2 carrots, peeled and shredded into thin matchsticks

3 tablespoons nutritional yeast

2 teaspoons garlic powder

½ teaspoon salt

½ teaspoon pepper

1. Wrap the tofu in paper towels and set it on a baking sheet. Place another sheet on top and a heavy object resting on the top sheet. Press the tofu until you are ready to fry.

2. In a small bowl, pour the boiling water over the mushrooms and soak for 10 minutes. Remove and discard any stems. Press the caps between paper towels to remove excess water.

3. In a saucepan, combine the soy sauce, mirin, and sugar. Set the heat on high and stir until the sugar dissolves. Bring the sauce to a boil for 2 minutes, then remove from the heat. Let cool before transferring it to a sauce bottle.

4. In a skillet, pour peanut oil into a pan until it is at least 2 inches deep. Place it over medium-high heat. Line a plate with paper towels and set a pair of tongs on top.

5. Pour the egg substitute into a small bowl. In a separate bowl, mix the flour and ½ cup of cornstarch until thoroughly blended.

6. When the oil reaches at least 375°F, or when a sprinkle of cornstarch bubbles immediately, it is ready. Working with one mushroom or asparagus piece at a time, dip it into the egg mixture, let it drip, toss it in the flour mixture until evenly coated, and then carefully place it in the oil. Repeat until you have 5 or 6 pieces in the oil.

7. When the pieces turn pale yellow, use tongs to transfer them to the paper towel–lined plate. They will turn golden brown while they are resting. Repeat steps 6 and 7 until all the mushrooms and asparagus are fried.

8. In a bowl, sprinkle some of the flour mixture over the shredded daikon and carrots. Toss with chopsticks until the shredded vegetables are evenly coated with the flour mixture. Pour some of the egg mixture into the bowl and toss again to evenly coat, then fry in small batches. With shredded vegetables, you want them to clump together in the oil and come out as a single fritter.

9. Cut the tofu into 1-inch cubes. In a small bowl, mix the remaining 4 tablespoons of cornstarch, nutritional yeast, garlic powder, salt, and pepper together in a small bowl. Toss each cube in the cornstarch mixture and then place in the oil. Take the tofu out once golden brown. Repeat until all the tofu is fried.

10. Assemble the tempura bowls, starting with a layer of rice and adding the tempura vegetables, tofu, and a light drizzle of sauce.

TIP: You can keep fried food hot by heating the oven to 200°F and placing a cooling rack on a baking sheet. The hot air needs to be able to reach all sides of the fried food.

VEGAN "TUNA" BEET POKE BOWL

MAKES 4 POKE BOWLS ✳ PREP TIME: 30 MINUTES PLUS 30 MINUTES MARINATING TIME

People either love or hate beets—there is very little in between. If you have fans of beets in your house, you're in luck, because this recipe is delicious! Brown rice, fresh vegetables, and marinated beets make this dish feel like "the real thing."

6 tablespoons soy sauce

1 tablespoon sesame seeds, toasted

2 tablespoons mirin

2 scallions, chopped

3 beets, cooked, peeled, and cut into ½-inch cubes

3 cups brown sushi rice

2 avocados, sliced

1 cucumber, cut into half moons

1 red bell pepper, cut into large matchsticks

4 ounces pickled daikon radish, cut into large matchsticks

2 half sheets nori, cut into 1/16-inch-wide strips (see tip)

½ cup Vegan Spicy Mayonnaise (page 108)

1. In a medium bowl, combine the soy sauce, sesame seeds, mirin, and scallions and mix well. Add the beets and toss until evenly coated. Store the marinated beets in a sealed container for at least 30 minutes (preferably overnight).

2. Assemble all the poke bowls simultaneously. For each bowl, start with a layer of rice. Place half an avocado, slices fanned out, along the edge of the bowl. Place a small handful of cucumber slices on the opposite edge from the avocado. Spoon ½ cup of marinated beets next to the avocado. Add a handful of bell pepper next to the cucumber.

3. Place a handful of pickled daikon next to the bell peppers and a large pinch of nori strips next to the beets. Add a generous dollop of spicy mayo in the center of each bowl and sprinkle any remaining scallions and/or sesame seeds on top.

TIP: Use a pair of kitchen scissors to cut the sheets of nori in half, lengthwise, and stack the strips. Starting at one end and working toward the other, cut strips of nori roughly 1/16 inch wide.

FULL OF FLORA CHIRASHI BOWL

MAKES 2 BOWLS ✳ PREP TIME: 40 MINUTES

There are plenty of hot days when I don't feel like cooking or even eating hot food. This recipe is one of my go-to solutions for those days because it doesn't require any of the ingredients to be cooked—except for the sushi rice, of course! 🥚 CONTAINS EGG

1 pound edamame, frozen

1 avocado

4 inari pouches

2 ounces Homemade Pickled Ginger (page 103 or store-bought)

2 cups sushi rice

8 ounces Tamago (page 111 or store-bought), cut into large matchsticks

2 ounces kimchi

1 yellow bell pepper, cut into large matchsticks

1 cucumber, cut into large matchsticks

1. Pour the frozen edamame into a large bowl and cover with hot water. Let thaw for 10 minutes. Remove the individual soybeans from the pods and put them in another bowl.

2. Slice the avocado into thin slices and fan them out on a plate. Slice the inari pouches into ¼-inch strips and set them on the plate with the avocado.

3. Use a mandoline to shave pickled ginger off the main root. Shave only as much as you need for each dish. Return the remaining ginger root to the pickling jar. (If you're using store-bought pickled ginger, skip this step.)

4. To assemble the chirashi bowls, start with a layer of sushi rice at the bottom of each bowl. Working from the outside edge of the rice inward, place 3 or 4 tamago slices, ½ avocado (slices fanned), inari, kimchi, pickled ginger, edamame, bell pepper, and, finally, cucumber. There is no specific order for the ingredients and the amount of each will vary according to preference. Build your chirashi bowl exactly the way you like it.

TIP: Vegan Spicy Mayonnaise (page 108), Garlic Mayonnaise (page 107), or Vegetarian Miso Mayonnaise (page 106) would be a welcome addition to this dish.

CHEATING DEATH SUSHI BOWL

MAKES 2 BOWLS ✳ PREP TIME: 2 HOURS 30 MINUTES ✳ COOK TIME: 30 MINUTES

Chirashi (scattered sushi) bowls are a great way to enjoy a lot of sushi for a fraction of the time it takes to prepare maki. Although this recipe calls for a considerable amount of time to pickle, marinate, and season the ingredients, the time it takes to slice and prepare the bowls is short. This recipe is also a tasty way to pack a bunch of nutrient-dense "superfoods" into one meal. ⊖ **CONTAINS EGG**

3 tablespoons sugar

2 teaspoons sea salt

½ teaspoon Japanese mustard (karashi)

2 cucumbers, Japanese or Persian, washed and trimmed

14 ounces extra-firm tofu

½ cup low-sodium soy sauce

2 tablespoons tomato paste

2 tablespoons maple syrup

2 tablespoons liquid smoke

3 tablespoons salted butter, melted

1 tablespoon brown sugar

2 cups sushi rice

1 avocado

1 jalapeño

Olive oil cooking spray

4 ounces wakame (seaweed salad)

Vegetarian Miso Mayonnaise (page 106)

Sesame seeds, toasted

TO MAKE THE BOWLS

1. Combine the sugar, salt, and Japanese mustard in a large resealable bag. Add the cucumbers and rub them with the sugar/salt mixture. Remove excess air from the bag and allow the cucumbers to pickle for at least 1 hour and up to 48 hours before using.

2. Drain the tofu and wrap it in paper towels or a clean cloth. Place it on a baking sheet with another baking sheet on top of the tofu. Set heavy objects on the top sheet to press excess moisture out. Let the tofu press for at least 1 hour, but preferably 2 hours.

3. In a small bowl, whisk together the soy sauce, tomato paste, maple syrup, liquid smoke, butter, and brown sugar. Pour the mixture into a sealable container. Slice the pressed tofu into ⅛-inch-thick matchsticks and add to the marinade. Marinate for 1 hour in the refrigerator.

4. Prepare your sushi rice and slice the avocado and jalapeño. Preheat the oven to 375°F.

5. Spray a baking sheet with cooking spray. Place the tofu sticks on the sheet and bake for 20 minutes. Spray the tops of the tofu with cooking spray and gently flip them over. Baste with some marinade and return to the oven for 15 minutes. Check every 5 minutes to avoid burning.

6. Remove the pickled cucumbers from the bag and discard the liquid. Without peeling, slice the cucumbers at an angle to get elongated disks. Store the cucumbers in a sealed container for up to 3 days in the refrigerator.

7. Assemble each sushi bowl by adding a layer of rice and placing the prepared ingredients on top. I prefer this order (starting at the top and working clockwise): cucumber, ½ avocado fanned out, tofu "bacon," jalapeño, wakame. If you use a small amount of each, you should get halfway around the bowl. You can repeat the pattern on the other half of the bowl for an aesthetically pleasing pattern.

8. Drizzle with miso mayo and sprinkle with sesame seeds.

TIP: Japanese or Persian cucumbers are ideal for this recipe because they have fewer seeds and tend to be crisper than regular cucumbers.

SPICY SEITAN AND BROWN RICE SUSHI BOWL

MAKES 2 BOWLS ✳ PREP TIME: 15 MINUTES ✳ COOK TIME: 30 MINUTES

Vegetarian chirashi bowls are great for using up leftover sushi ingredients. This sushi bowl recipe has the added nutritional benefit of brown rice. This is the perfect recipe for a sweet, spicy, savory, and incredibly satisfying meal for two. Feel free to add or substitute your favorite ingredients. 🥚 CONTAINS EGG

2 cups brown sushi rice

½ cup soy sauce

3 tablespoons brown sugar

1 tablespoon
nutritional yeast

1 garlic clove, grated

1½-inch piece fresh
ginger, grated

1 teaspoon red
pepper flakes

8 ounces seitan strips

1 avocado

1 carrot

4 ounces Tamago (page 111
or store-bought)

2 half sheets nori

1 tablespoon sesame oil

4 ounces kimchi

Sesame seeds

1. While the rice is cooking, combine the soy sauce, brown sugar, nutritional yeast, garlic, ginger, and red pepper flakes in a small bowl. Add the seitan and marinate for at least 20 minutes.

2. Slice the avocado, carrot, tamago, and nori.

3. Heat the oil in a large pan and add the seitan. Once the seitan has browned on two sides, add the remaining marinade and simmer for 5 to 7 minutes, until the water has evaporated.

4. When the rice is cooked, portion it into two bowls and add the following to each bowl: avocado, carrots, tamago, nori, and kimchi.

5. Add a generous portion of seitan and sprinkle with sesame seeds.

TIP: Pair sweet and spicy seitan with a dry beer, like Sapporo, or a white wine, like Riesling.

DYNAMITE SUSHI TOWER

MAKES 6 TOWERS ✳ PREP TIME: 45 MINUTES ✳ COOK TIME: 1 HOUR

Sushi towers are easy to make and allow a ton of creative ingredients to be used. Each sushi restaurant will use a different mold to make their sushi towers (3-inch baking rings, thin cake collars, etc.), but your sushi tower doesn't need to be perfectly vertical on the sides. Plenty of people use cups or bowls to mold and stack their sushi towers and the results can be incredible.

Peanut oil or vegetable oil,
  for frying
1 cup egg substitute,
  whisked
1 cup cornstarch
2 cups king oyster
  mushrooms, cut into
  ½-inch cubes
½ cup Vegan Spicy
  Mayonnaise (page 108)
6 sheets nori
2 cups sushi rice
1 avocado, cut into
  ½-inch cubes
1 cup wakame
  (seaweed salad)
Sesame seeds, for garnish
  (optional)

1. Pour the oil into a cast-iron skillet over high heat. Pour the egg substitute into one bowl and the cornstarch into a separate bowl. Line a plate with paper towels or set out a wire rack.

2. Test the temperature of the oil by sprinkling cornstarch into the oil; if it starts to sizzle, it's ready. Toss a small handful of mushrooms into the egg substitute and coat them evenly. Allow the excess to drip off and then dip them in the cornstarch. Carefully lower the coated mushrooms into the oil, using tongs or a skimmer, and fry until golden brown.

3. Transfer the mushrooms to the prepared plate or wire rack. Repeat with the remaining mushrooms until all have been fried.

4. Transfer the mushrooms to a large bowl and toss with the spicy mayo. Set aside.

5. Use kitchen scissors to cut the nori sheets to the desired size and shape of your sushi tower mold. Place the mold over one piece of nori and add a thick layer of rice to the mold, pressing gently to pack.

CONTINUED

DYNAMITE SUSHI TOWER (CONTINUED)

6. Add a layer of avocado cubes to the mold, gently pressing. Add another layer of sushi rice and then a layer of wakame.

7. Gently slide the mold up and off the sushi tower. Use a spatula to transfer the tower to a plate. Take a small handful of fried mushrooms and place them carefully on top of the tower. Garnish with additional mayo and sprinkle with sesame seeds, if using.

8. Repeat steps 5 through 7 to make five more towers.

TIP: Keep an eye on the temperature of the oil when frying. Using a thermometer is ideal, but you can also monitor the temperature by timing how long it takes to cook the mushrooms. If the time decreases, your oil is getting too hot; if the time increases, the oil is getting too cool.

TERIYAKI TEMPEH SUSHI TOWER

MAKES 6 TOWERS ✳ PREP TIME: 25 MINUTES ✳ COOK TIME: 20 MINUTES

It turns out that honey, garlic, and teriyaki sauce are the key components for this crunchy, delicious vegetarian sushi tower. Skip the chopsticks and go straight for the forks with this dish—you'll be grateful that you did. You'll need a 3-inch-diameter baking ring or something similar.

2 tablespoons sesame oil, divided

8 ounces tempeh, cut into squares

2 tablespoons honey

2 tablespoons water

1 tablespoon low-sodium soy sauce

2 tablespoons teriyaki sauce

3 garlic cloves, minced

6 sheets nori

2 cups sushi rice

1 avocado, chopped into cubes

2 carrots, peeled and cut into thin coins

9 ounces spinach, cooked and squeezed well

TIP: Tongs and kitchen tweezers are great, but cooking chopsticks are better! These can be used when panfrying, grilling, mixing, and even garnishing your food.

1. Heat 1 tablespoon of oil in a skillet over medium-high heat and add the tempeh. Cook until golden brown on each side. Set aside on a plate.

2. In a small bowl, mix together the honey, water, soy sauce, and teriyaki sauce.

3. In a small saucepan, heat the remaining 1 tablespoon of oil. Add the garlic and fry for 60 seconds or until fragrant.

4. Add the sauce to the garlic and cook for 2 to 3 minutes to thicken. Add the seared tempeh and toss to evenly coat. Cook for 2 minutes and set aside.

5. Using kitchen scissors, cut the nori to the desired size and shape of your sushi tower mold. Place the mold over one piece of nori and add a thick layer of rice to the mold, pressing it gently to pack.

6. Add a generous layer of tempeh and cover with a thick layer of avocado. Each layer should be about 1 inch thick, if not a little more. Add a thin layer of overlapping carrots and pile one-sixth of the spinach on top.

7. Gently slide the mold up and off the sushi tower. Use a spatula to transfer your sushi tower to a plate.

8. Repeat steps 5 through 7 to make five more towers.

SWEET AND SOUR MINI SUSHI TOWERS

MAKES 10 TO 12 MINI TOWERS ✳ PREP TIME: 25 MINUTES

This sweet and sour sushi tower is a great way to cool down on a hot day. It's colorful, refreshing, and filled with flavor. This is a really fun dish to bring to a party, but it must be assembled when you arrive. The sheets of seaweed help transfer the mini sushi tower from the platter to the guest's plate and add aesthetic appeal.

2 fresh mangos, cubed

¼ red onion, diced

1 tablespoon cilantro, chopped

1 tablespoon toasted sesame seeds

½ tablespoon mirin

Juice of ½ lime

½ tablespoon soy sauce

1 avocado

2 cups sushi rice

1 cucumber, cut into thin coins

6 tablespoons vegan tobiko (See Vegan Tobiko Gunkan Maki, page 67)

3 half sheets nori

1. In a bowl, combine the mango, onion, cilantro, sesame seeds, and mirin. Add the lime juice and soy sauce. Stir until everything is evenly coated and mixed. Let the mixture sit for at least 15 minutes.

2. Halve the avocado and remove the pit. Peel the avocado by hand and chop roughly into cubes.

3. Set a 3-inch biscuit cutter on a serving plate. Place a ½-inch-thick layer of rice and avocado in the base. Add a thin layer of cucumber and another ½-inch layer of rice. Spoon a generous amount of mango mixture on top of the tower.

4. Carefully slide the mold up and off the tower and add about 1 tablespoon of tobiko.

5. Repeat steps 3 and 4 to make the remaining mini towers.

6. Cut the nori sheets in half and then cut each half into triangles. Wrap one triangle around each mini sushi tower.

TIP: Avoid the biscuit cutters that have handles that go over the top. The handle gets in the way of ingredient placement more than it helps remove the mold.

TOFU MUSUBI

MAKES 8 PIECES ✳ PREP TIME: 1 HOUR ✳ COOK TIME: 30 MINUTES

Musubi is originally made from Spam, but in this recipe, we use tofu to make Hawaii's favorite snack. The key to flavorful tofu is marinating it overnight and then baking it. Although it's possible to get great-tasting tofu faster than that, this is my preferred way to cook tofu.

14 ounces extra-firm tofu

½ cup vegetable broth

¼ cup low-sodium
   soy sauce

1 teaspoon mirin

¼ cup maple syrup

1 tablespoon liquid smoke

2 garlic cloves, grated

1-inch-piece of fresh
   ginger, grated

2 cups sushi rice

8 half sheets nori

1. Drain the tofu and wrap it in paper towels or a clean cloth. Place it on a baking sheet with another baking sheet on top of the tofu. Set heavy objects on the top sheet to press excess moisture out. Let the tofu press for at least 30 minutes, but preferably 2 hours.

2. In a resealable container, combine the broth, soy sauce, mirin, maple syrup, liquid smoke, garlic, and ginger. Stir until well blended.

3. Once the tofu is pressed, discard the liquid, and cut the tofu into 4 equal slices (about the size of a slice of Spam). Add the tofu to the marinade and let it soak for at least 30 minutes, but preferably overnight.

4. Preheat the oven to 400°F. Line a baking sheet with parchment paper and place the marinated tofu slices on the sheet a few inches apart. Bake for 15 minutes, then flip and baste with marinade on the other side. Bake for an additional 10 to 15 minutes (check every 5 minutes to make sure they don't burn).

5. Form the rice into 1-inch-thick rectangles that closely match the shape and size of the tofu slices. You can skip this step if you have a musubi press.

CONTINUED

Sashimi, Chirashi, Nigiri, Inari, and Other Sushi

TOFU MUSUBI (CONTINUED)

6. Cut the nori sheets in half lengthwise. Place one strip on the cutting board and place a piece of tofu on top. If you have a musubi press, place the press on the tofu before adding rice. If you don't have a press, place a rice rectangle on top of the tofu. Wrap a nori strip around the tofu and rice and seal on the bottom using a few grains of smashed rice as a paste.

7. Repeat step 6 to make seven more musubi.

TIP: It's not required to use a musubi press, but it definitely makes the process go a lot faster!

SEITAN MUSUBI

MAKES 8 PIECES ✳ PREP TIME: 30 MINUTES ✳ COOK TIME: 1 HOUR

Seitan is great because it can look and taste just like real meat. Store-bought seitan usually comes in small nuggets or strips, but to make musubi, we need large slices, which is why we're making our own seitan for this recipe. A rich soup is important because seitan absorbs flavors wonderfully. You're welcome to experiment with the soup ingredients, but I encourage you to try this version first.

1 cup vital wheat gluten

¼ cup chickpea flour

2 cups water, divided

5 cups vegetable broth

1 (4-inch-by-4-inch) piece kombu

2 tablespoons awase miso paste (see page 3)

2 tablespoons maple syrup

2 tablespoons rice wine vinegar

2 tablespoons nutritional yeast

4 tablespoons soy sauce

2 teaspoons liquid smoke

2 teaspoons paprika

1 teaspoon onion powder

2 teaspoons garlic power

2 cups sushi rice

2 half sheets nori

6 tablespoons teriyaki sauce

1 tablespoon vegetable oil

1. Combine the vital wheat gluten and chickpea flour in a bowl. Add 1 cup of water and form a dough. Transfer to a flat surface and knead the dough for 5 minutes, then set aside to rest for at least 5 minutes.

2. In a large pot, combine the broth, remaining 1 cup of water, kombu, miso paste, maple syrup, vinegar, nutritional yeast, soy sauce, liquid smoke, paprika, onion powder, and garlic powder and bring to a boil. Once the mixture boils, reduce the heat to a simmer. Cut the dough into 8 pieces (larger pieces may not cook thoroughly).

3. Add the dough to the broth and cook for 1 hour, making sure the broth doesn't come to a boil. Use tongs to flip the seitan periodically to ensure even cooking. Once the seitan is done cooking, remove it from the broth and allow to cool.

4. Prepare the sushi rice and cut the nori in half lengthwise.

5. Cut the seitan into ⅛-inch-thick slices and baste each slice with the teriyaki sauce. Place a skillet over high heat with the vegetable oil. Sear the seitan for 2 to 3 minutes on each side, until the sauce is caramelized.

CONTINUED

SEITAN MUSUBI (CONTINUED)

6. Form the rice into 8 (1-inch-thick) rectangles that closely match the slices of seitan in size and shape. (Skip this step if you have a musubi press.)

7. Place one nori strip on the cutting board and place a slice of seitan on top. (If you have a musubi press, place the press on top of the seitan before adding rice.) Place a rice rectangle on top of the seitan. Wrap the seaweed around the tofu and rice and seal on the bottom using a few grains of smashed rice as a paste.

8. Repeat step 7 to make seven more musubi.

TIP: You can use the leftover broth from cooking the seitan as a soup base. It tastes great with chopped seitan, rice, and vegetables. It may be a little salty, but you can add water or vegetable broth to adjust it to your taste.

SPINACH AND TAMAGO OSHIZUSHI

MAKES 8 PIECES ✳ PREP TIME: 10 MINUTES

Oshizushi is an easy way to make sushi without having to worry about rolling or using seaweed. Traditionally, this form of sushi was limited to two or three ingredients, but you can incorporate more as you become familiar with making oshizushi at home. This recipe requires an oshizushi press (or *oshibako*, a box-shaped press) as there is no feasible way to achieve the same amount of pressure without it.

⌁ CONTAINS EGG

1 cup sushi rice

3 tablespoons furikake

1 pound spinach

14 ounces Tamago (page 111 or store-bought), sliced

1. Prepare the sushi rice and add the furikake after the rice has been seasoned but before it completely cools.

2. If using a wooden oshibako, soak the pieces (top lid, sides, and bottom lid) in cold water for 10 minutes.

3. Bring a small pot of water to a rolling boil and add the spinach. Boil for 40 seconds, then immediately run the spinach under cold water. Once the spinach is cool to the touch, squeeze as much water out as possible. You can place it in a clean dish towel and gather the sides to form a seal. Twist repeatedly to wring out more water.

4. Assemble the oshibako so the sides are resting on the bottom lid. Place a generous layer of spinach (about ½ inch) inside the box. Next, add a thin layer of rice and place a few tamago slices on top. Finally, add another thin layer of rice to fill the box.

CONTINUED

SPINACH AND TAMAGO OSHIZUSHI (CONTINUED)

5. Set the top lid on the ingredients and slowly start to press down. Once the lid is partway down the sides, you can increase the pressure on it to ensure that the ingredients are compressed evenly. You might need to press harder than you initially thought! Go hard.

6. To remove the oshibako, keep your thumbs on the top lid while using your fingers to slowly pull the sides up. Remove the top lid and carefully flip the oshizushi over onto your cutting board. Now the bottom lid should be on top of the sushi.

7. Remove the bottom lid and slice the sushi into 8 even pieces.

TIP: Wooden oshibako are preferred over plastic because they are easier to use, but they are harder to keep clean. Don't wash an oshibako in the dishwasher; it isn't able to dry quickly and will get moldy.

VEGAN OSHIZUSHI

MAKES 8 PIECES ✳ PREP TIME: 20 MINUTES ✳ COOK TIME: 15 MINUTES

Oshizushi is predominantly seafood-based, but recently people have been asking for more vegetarian and vegan options. You can use any vegetable and preparation method you choose, as long as the ingredients are not too liquid-y. Liquid squeezing out while pressing the sushi will result in rice that doesn't stick together. This recipe requires the use of an oshibako.

2 tablespoons unsalted
  vegan butter, melted
1 tablespoon soy sauce
1 teaspoon honey
1 garlic clove, grated
1 tablespoon oil, plus more
  for brushing
4 to 6 ounces king oyster
  mushrooms, sliced
1 cup sushi rice
1 cucumber, sliced
1 carrot, peeled and
  thinly shaved

1. If using a wooden oshibako, soak the pieces (top lid, sides, bottom lid) in cold water for 10 minutes. Dry off the pieces.

2. In a small bowl, stir together the butter, soy sauce, honey, and garlic until well blended.

3. Heat the oil in a nonstick skillet over medium-high heat. Working in batches if necessary, arrange the mushrooms in the pan so they don't touch. Brush additional oil over the mushrooms as they cook. Panfry the mushrooms for 5 minutes on each side.

4. Once the mushrooms are cooked, add the sauce and remove the skillet from the heat. Toss the mushroom pieces in the sauce until evenly coated. Leave the mushrooms in the pan for at least 5 minutes to absorb the sauce.

5. Assemble the oshibako so the sides are resting on the bottom lid. Place a layer of mushrooms in the box. Next, add a thin layer of rice and place a few cucumber slices on top. Add another thin layer of rice and top with carrot strips, then cover with rice again. This should fill the oshibako.

CONTINUED

VEGAN OSHIZUSHI

6. Set the top lid on the ingredients and slowly start to press down. Once the lid is partway down the sides, you can increase the pressure on it to ensure that the ingredients are compressed evenly. You might need to press harder than you initially thought.

7. To remove the oshibako, keep your thumbs on the top lid while using your fingers to slowly pull the sides up. Remove the top lid and carefully flip the oshizushi over onto your cutting board. Now the bottom lid should be on top of the sushi.

8. Remove the bottom lid and slice the sushi into 8 even pieces.

AVOCADO RADISH TEMARI

MAKES 8 PIECES ❋ PREP TIME: 20 MINUTES

Temari, or temarizushi, is probably the easiest form of sushi to make at home. It is named after the traditional Japanese craft of making colorful hand balls out of embroidered fabric. Although this form of sushi uses a limited number of ingredients, the possibilities are almost endless. This recipe features savory avocado paired with sharp radish to balance flavor with texture.

1 avocado

2 small radishes, washed and trimmed

1 cup sushi rice

TIP: For this type of roll, it takes practice to make the toppings look symmetrical and/or aligned. Keep trying and you'll soon get the hang of it!

1. Drape an 8-inch piece of plastic wrap over a small bowl. Set a bowl of water on the counter.

2. Peel the avocado, cut it in half, and remove the pit. Place the flat side of each half facedown and pointing left to right on a cutting board. Place the tip of a sharp knife on the cutting board above the avocado and draw the knife tip through it (never letting the tip leave the cutting board). Use this technique to slice the avocado into very thin slices.

3. Using a similar technique, slice the radishes as thinly as possible. The slices should be flexible and almost translucent.

4. Fan out 3 or 4 radish slices and place them on the plastic wrap over the bowl. Fan out the same number of avocado slices and place them next to the radish slices. With slightly wet hands, roll about 2 tablespoons of rice into a small ball. Place the rice ball on top of the ingredients.

5. Gather the plastic wrap around the ingredients and twist the top to seal them inside. Gently form the temari using your hands until you have the desired ball shape. Unwrap the temari and place it on a plate.

6. Repeat steps 4 and 5 to make seven more temari.

OSHINKO SPINACH TEMARI

MAKES 8 PIECES ✳ PREP TIME: 20 MINUTES ✳ COOK TIME: 15 MINUTES

Temari make appealing appetizers for any party. These balls of sushi can be themed to match the party, they are easy to transport, and they don't require utensils or any additional sauce. This recipe features rich spinach leaves and bright oshinko pickles, resulting in colorful, flavorful, and crunchy bite-size pieces of sushi.

9 to 12 ounces spinach leaves, blanched

2 ounces takuan (aka oshinko, pickled daikon radish)

1 cup sushi rice

1. Drape an 8-inch piece of plastic wrap over a small bowl. Set a bowl of water on the counter.

2. Bring a small pot of water to a rolling boil. Add the spinach and boil for 45 seconds before running it under cold water to stop the cooking process immediately. Once the spinach is cool to the touch, squeeze as much water out as possible. You can place it in a clean dish towel and gather the sides to form a seal. Twist repeatedly to wring out more water.

3. Halve the takuan lengthwise. The cross section should look like a half moon. Place the tip of your knife on the cutting board just above the takuan. Without letting the knife tip leave the cutting board, draw a straight line through the takuan to make a thin slice. Repeat this technique to slice the takuan into thin, flexible pieces.

4. Fan out 3 or 4 takuan slices and place on the plastic wrap over the bowl. Grab a small chunk of spinach and open it up so the leaves lie somewhat flat. Place the spinach next to the takuan slices. With slightly wet hands, roll about 2 tablespoons of rice into a small ball. Place the rice ball on top of the ingredients.

5. Gather the plastic wrap around the ingredients and twist the top to seal them inside. Gently form the temari using your hands until you have the desired ball shape. Unwrap the temari and place on a plate.

6. Repeat steps 4 and 5 to make seven more temari.

TIP: Temari are easy to "dress up" with sauce and/or sprinkled ingredients on top. Don't be afraid to get creative!

Sides and Sauces

VEGAN MISO SOUP

SERVES 4 ✳ PREP TIME: 20 MINUTES ✳ COOK TIME: 15 MINUTES

Miso soup is the quintessential sushi appetizer in the Western part of the world, but in Japan, miso soup is more commonly eaten as a finale to the dinner. Most miso soup recipes contain *dashi* (fish stock) so they don't qualify as vegan. This recipe was made for vegans but doesn't compromise on flavor.

4 cups water, divided
8 shiitake mushrooms
1 (4-by-4-inch) piece kombu
3 tablespoons miso paste
3 tablespoons
  dried wakame
14 ounces firm tofu
2 scallions, sliced

TIP: Miso soup is rejuvenating! It's great for upset stomachs and general fatigue. Miso soup can be refrigerated in a sealed container for up to three days and reheated on the stovetop.

1. In a small saucepan, boil 1 cup of water. Put the mushrooms into a medium bowl and, when the water is boiling, pour it over the mushrooms. Let them soak for at least 10 minutes. Remove the shiitake mushrooms and reserve the water. Slice the mushrooms in half and discard any stems.

2. In a saucepan, bring the remaining 3 cups of water to a gentle simmer and add the kombu. Allow the kombu to steep for 10 minutes before removing and discarding it. Add the shiitake mushroom water to the kombu water to create a vegan dashi.

3. In a separate saucepan, combine the miso paste and wakame. Stir gently over medium heat, making sure the mixture doesn't come to a boil, until the miso paste has completely dissolved.

4. Dice the tofu into cubes. The size of the cubes is up to you, but traditionally the cubes are ¼ inch thick. Add the tofu, mushrooms, scallions, and wakame mixture to the dashi. Cook for another 10 minutes before serving. You can keep miso soup warm over low heat for several hours. Be sure to stir the pot periodically, as miso soup tends to settle.

JAPANESE HOUSE SALAD WITH TRADITIONAL GINGER DRESSING

MAKES ABOUT 2½ CUPS ✳ PREP TIME: 20 MINUTES

Most store-bought Japanese ginger dressings taste different from what you experience at restaurants because restaurants generally make their own (and they generally don't use preservatives). Each restaurant varies their ingredients to suit the taste of their customers, but this recipe is my personal favorite. The core ingredients for traditional ginger dressing are carrots, peanut oil, and celery, which really fill out the dressing and give it that fresh, crisp taste.

FOR THE DRESSING

1 large carrot, peeled
  and chopped
½ cup diced white onion
½ teaspoon minced garlic
3 tablespoons grated
  ginger root
½ cup peanut oil
1 cup diced celery
⅓ cup rice wine vinegar
2 tablespoons water
1 cup sliced tomato
4 teaspoons soy sauce
2 teaspoons sugar
2 teaspoons lemon juice
½ teaspoon salt
¼ teaspoon freshly ground
  black pepper
1½ tablespoons sesame oil

FOR THE SALAD

Salad greens
1 cucumber, sliced
1 carrot, peeled and sliced
1 avocado, sliced
Cherry tomatoes

1. **To make the dressing:** In a food processor or blender, combine the carrot, onion, garlic, ginger, peanut oil, celery, vinegar, water, tomato, soy sauce, sugar, lemon juice, salt, pepper, and sesame oil and blend until the consistency is to your liking. Store in a jar or sauce bottle until you're ready to use it.

2. **To make the salad:** In a large bowl, combine the salad greens, cucumber, carrot, avocado, and cherry tomatoes and toss well. Drizzle the ginger dressing on top and enjoy!

TIP: Because there are no preservatives in this salad dressing, it is good for only three days.

EDAMAME

SERVES 6 ✳ COOK TIME: 15 MINUTES

Edamame is a fantastic vegan appetizer that goes well with almost any Asian dish. Edamame is easy to find in stores, fast to prepare, and fun to eat. You can experiment with different seasonings or go with the classic flaky salt sprinkled on top. I like to add a little heat with Japanese seven spice because it's not so hot that kids won't eat it, but it is spicy enough to notice.

Edamame, frozen, shell on
Flaky salt
Nanami togarashi
  (Japanese seven spice)

1. Pour the frozen edamame into a large bowl. Cover the edamame completely with boiling water and allow it to sit for 10 minutes.

2. Carefully pour out the water, season to taste with salt and nanami togarashi, and serve.

TIP: Keep several bags of frozen edamame for unexpected guests or short-notice party appetizers. Store any remaining edamame in a sealed container in the refrigerator for up to five days.

HOMEMADE PICKLED GINGER

MAKES ABOUT 2 CUPS ❋ PREP TIME: 10 MINUTES PLUS 1 WEEK TO MARINATE

Pickled ginger is easy to prepare at home and tastes significantly better without the added food coloring, artificial sweeteners, and extra preservatives in commercial pickled ginger. Fresh ginger will naturally turn slightly pink; in fact, the fresher the ginger, the pinker it will become, whereas ginger root that has been stored for weeks will not turn pink at all. Once your ginger has been pickled, it will keep for several months.

6 to 8 ounces fresh ginger root
2 teaspoons salt
1 cup rice wine vinegar
½ cup water
3 tablespoons sugar

1. Peel the ginger root by holding a butter knife perpendicular to the skin and scraping it off. (Ginger skin is surprisingly soft and peels too easily for a standard vegetable peeler. Most vegetable peelers would remove too much ginger.)

2. Rub the salt gently onto the ginger root and let it rest for 24 hours.

3. In a bowl, mix together the vinegar, water, and sugar until the sugar has completely dissolved. Rinse the ginger root and place it in an empty jar. Pour the mixture into the jar and let the ginger marinate for at least 1 week in a cool, dark place.

TIP: When ready to eat, slice only as much as you think you'll need.

VEGETARIAN GYOZA

MAKES 35 TO 40 PIECES ✳ PREP TIME: 1 HOUR 30 MINUTES ✳ COOK TIME: 15 MINUTES

Gyoza, or pot stickers, are one of my favorite appetizers for sushi. The combination of the crispy wonton wrapper with the steamed filling creates a delightfully satisfying bite. I always serve gyoza with light soy sauce and a few drops of chili oil or sriracha for added heat. There are hundreds of variations of pot stickers from several different countries, so feel free to modify this recipe or add ingredients to your liking.

6 ounces firm tofu

3 ounces cabbage

Salt

1-inch knob fresh ginger

1 garlic clove

1 ounce yellow onion

2 ounces carrot

3 ounces shiitake
mushroom caps

1 tablespoon soy sauce

2 teaspoons toasted
sesame oil, plus more
for frying

½ tablespoon awase miso
paste (see page 3)

⅛ teaspoon ground
white pepper

1 tablespoon cornstarch

40 to 50 round gyoza
wrappers (wonton
wrappers)

1. Drain the tofu and wrap it in paper towels or a clean cloth. Place it on a baking sheet with another baking sheet on top of the tofu. Set heavy objects on the top sheet to press excess moisture out. Let the tofu press for at least 30 minutes, but preferably 2 hours.

2. Slice the cabbage into ¼-inch strips and rub a generous amount of salt into the strips. Let the cabbage rest for at least 30 minutes. After 30 minutes, wring out the cabbage with your hands and dice it into small squares.

3. Grate the ginger and garlic into a large bowl. Dice the onion, carrot, and mushrooms and add them to the bowl. Add the cabbage.

4. In a small bowl, thoroughly mix the soy sauce, sesame oil, miso paste, and white pepper together.

5. Slice the tofu into small cubes, about the same size as the vegetables. Add the tofu and sauce to the large bowl and carefully mix everything together to coat with sauce. Sprinkle with the cornstarch to help prevent the mixture from being too wet.

6. Set a small bowl of water on the counter. Working with one gyoza wrapper at a time, dip one finger into the water and wet the edge of the wrapper, tracing the edge in a circular motion.

7. Place the wrapper in the palm of your nondominant hand. Use a 1-tablespoon measuring spoon to place a scoop of vegetable mixture onto the center of the wrapper. It's best to start with less filling and work your way up to using more.

8. Fold the wrapper in half and pinch the two wet edges together in the center. The gyoza should be in the shape of a half circle. Use your thumb and index finger to form pleats on the side closest to you, one pleat about every quarter inch.

9. Repeat to make pleats on the other half of the wrapper. After all the pleats have been made, press them together to seal the gyoza completely.

10. Repeat steps 6 through 9 to assemble all the gyoza.

11. Pour oil into a skillet and put it over medium heat. Once the pan is hot, place the desired amount of gyoza in the pan. Cook until the bottoms of the gyoza are golden brown.

12. Add ¼ cup of water to the pan and cover with a lid. Steam the gyoza for at least 3 minutes before removing the lid. Once the lid is removed, allow the remaining water to evaporate.

TIP: You can freeze gyoza. Once removed from the freezer, steam them for 2 minutes longer than you would fresh gyoza.

VEGETARIAN MISO MAYONNAISE

MAKES ABOUT 1 CUP ✳ PREP TIME: 10 MINUTES

Miso mayo is a quick and easy way to add umami to any dish. There are a few different types of miso paste to choose from. White miso paste is subtle and can easily go unnoticed, whereas red miso paste can be overpowering with its bold notes. You can use any type of miso for this recipe, but I recommend *awase* (combination) because it supplies the best from both types. ⊙ **CONTAINS EGG**

1 cup real mayonnaise
⅛ cup miso paste (red or combination)
2 tablespoons mirin
1 teaspoon soy sauce
½ teaspoon sesame oil

In a small bowl, combine the mayonnaise, miso paste, mirin, soy sauce, and sesame oil. Whisk vigorously until thoroughly combined. Carefully pour the sauce into a sauce bottle and store in the refrigerator for up to 2 weeks.

TIP: You can try vegan mayonnaise for this sauce, but from experience, the recipe doesn't work nearly as well as it does with real mayonnaise.

GARLIC MAYONNAISE

MAKES ABOUT ½ CUP ✳ PREP TIME: 10 MINUTES

This sauce is the perfect blend of sweet and savory, combining the richness of Japanese mayonnaise with garlic, honey, and a splash of lemon juice. This is my favorite sauce to use on vegetarian and vegan sushi. Kewpie, the specific brand of mayonnaise called for, uses a small amount of MSG, so please be aware of any MSG sensitivities when making this recipe. For best results, don't substitute any ingredients. ◌ **CONTAINS EGG**

½ cup Kewpie mayonnaise

1 teaspoon lemon juice

2 tablespoons honey

1 teaspoon garlic powder

½ teaspoon ichimi togarashi (Japanese chili powder)

In a small bowl, combine the mayonnaise, lemon juice, honey, garlic powder, and ichimi togarashi. Whisk vigorously until thoroughly combined. Carefully pour the sauce into a sauce bottle and store in the refrigerator for up to 2 weeks.

TIP: This recipe makes a small amount, but you can easily scale up the ingredients if you need to make more.

VEGAN SPICY MAYONNAISE

MAKES ABOUT 1 CUP ✳ PREP TIME: 5 MINUTES

This is the most common sushi sauce to make at home because it's one of the easiest to make. There are numerous variations of spicy mayo, but this one is my favorite. This is a great sauce to have on hand, even if you're not planning on making sushi. I've seen people use spicy mayo on sandwiches and salads, with french fries, and on pizza.

1 cup vegan mayonnaise

3 tablespoons sriracha

1 teaspoon sesame oil

1 teaspoon nanami togarashi (Japanese seven spice)

Combine the vegan mayonnaise, sriracha, sesame oil, and nanami togarashi in a bowl and whisk until thoroughly mixed. Pour the spicy mayo into an empty sauce bottle and store in the refrigerator for up to 2 weeks.

TIP: Sesame oil adds depth to the flavor. You can add more or less sriracha, but don't leave out the oil!

TEMPURA VEGGIE APPETIZER

SERVES 4 ✳ PREP TIME: 40 MINUTES ✳ COOK TIME: 30 MINUTES

Deep-frying food isn't unique to Japanese cuisine, but the way tempura fried food stands out is due to the details. The secret to light, crunchy tempura comes from using extremely cold water to make the batter. The more extreme the temperature difference between the batter and the oil, the better. Peanut oil has a higher smoking point than most other oils, so I recommend using it in this recipe. ⌂ CONTAINS EGG

8 to 12 shiitake mushrooms

2 carrots

1 sweet potato

8 asparagus stalks

4 okra pods

1 eggplant

1 green bell pepper

1 yellow onion

1 (4-by-4-inch) piece kombu

½ cup soy sauce

½ cup mirin

1 egg, beaten

1 cup ice-cold water

1 cup all-purpose
   flour, sifted

Peanut oil

1. Bring 2 cups of water to a boil in a small pot. Once boiling, add the mushrooms and turn off the heat. Place a lid on the pot and soak the mushrooms for 20 minutes. Meanwhile, slice the carrots, sweet potato, asparagus, okra, eggplant, bell pepper, and onion into ¼-inch strips.

2. Remove the mushrooms from the pot and add the kombu to the water. Turn down the heat so the water barely simmers for 10 minutes. Remove and discard the kombu. Add the soy sauce and mirin. Bring to a boil for 2 minutes and then allow the dipping sauce to cool naturally.

3. Remove and discard the mushroom stems. Press the caps between paper towels to remove excess water. You don't want a lot of water in the ingredients you're about to deep fry.

4. To make the batter, combine the egg and water in a bowl. Mix them together really well and then add the flour. Mix the flour into the egg wash, but don't whisk; the batter should be significantly clumpy. Add 3 ice cubes and put the batter in the refrigerator until the oil is hot enough to fry in.

CONTINUED

5. Fill a large skillet with 2 inches of oil and place over medium-high heat. When the oil reaches at least 375°F, it's ready. Line a plate with paper towels.

6. Lightly coat each vegetable piece in flour and then dip it into the batter. Allow excess batter to drip off before gently placing the pieces in the oil. Fry 3 to 4 pieces at a time to prevent the oil from cooling down.

7. Remove each piece when it turns golden but before it starts to darken. Transfer the pieces to the paper towel–lined plate or a wire rack. The color should deepen while cooling. Repeat steps 6 and 7 until all the vegetables have been tempura-fried.

8. Serve with a small dish of dipping sauce, preferably while both are still warm.

TIP: The batter needs to have a clumpy texture to achieve the right effect. Do not whisk the batter!

TAMAGO (JAPANESE OMELET)

SERVES 4 ✳ PREP TIME: 25 MINUTES ✳ COOK TIME: 20 MINUTES

Making your own tamago can seem daunting, but don't let it discourage you! If you decide to opt for store-bought tamago, be sure to read the ingredients list, as most tamago recipes contain fish products.
◠ CONTAINS EGG

1 (3-by-3-inch) piece kombu

2 tablespoons mirin

1 teaspoon soy sauce

1 teaspoon powdered sugar

1 teaspoon salt

6 large eggs, beaten

Vegetable oil

1. Start by making the kombu dashi, or seaweed stock. Bring 1½ cups of water to a boil in a pot and add the kombu. Immediately reduce the heat so that the water is barely simmering. Allow the kombu to cook for 10 minutes. Remove and discard the kombu. While you wait, wrap a bamboo rolling mat in plastic film.

2. In a bowl, combine 3 tablespoons of the kombu dashi, the mirin, soy sauce, sugar, and salt. Add this mixture to the beaten eggs and stir well.

3. Place a skillet over medium heat. Soak a paper towel in vegetable oil and use it to lightly coat the pan. Add roughly one-fourth of the egg mixture to the pan and tilt the pan around to get a thin, even layer.

4. Once the egg starts to set, use a spatula to roll up the omelet toward you. Keeping the rolled omelet in the pan, push it back to the farthest side. Oil the empty portion of the pan and then pour in more egg mixture. Lift the rolled omelet up and tilt the pan to allow the egg mixture to run underneath the rolled omelet. Once the egg mixture looks halfway cooked, start rolling the omelet toward you again. Repeat this step until you have used all the egg mixture.

5. Slide the omelet on to the rolling mat. Roll the omelet carefully into the center of the mat and then firmly wrap the mat around the omelet. Use rubber bands or string to bind the mat around the omelet. Tip the mat up so the tamago is standing on one end, and let it cool for at least 5 minutes before removing the mat. This will help the egg layers bind together and keep the tamago compressed.

MEASUREMENT CONVERSIONS

VOLUME EQUIVALENTS	U.S. STANDARD	U.S. STANDARD (OUNCES)	METRIC (APPROXIMATE)
LIQUID	2 tablespoons	1 fl. oz.	30 mL
	¼ cup	2 fl. oz.	60 mL
	½ cup	4 fl. oz.	120 mL
	1 cup	8 fl. oz.	240 mL
	1½ cups	12 fl. oz.	355 mL
	2 cups or 1 pint	16 fl. oz.	475 mL
	4 cups or 1 quart	32 fl. oz.	1 L
	1 gallon	128 fl. oz.	4 L
DRY	⅛ teaspoon	—	0.5 mL
	¼ teaspoon	—	1 mL
	½ teaspoon	—	2 mL
	¾ teaspoon	—	4 mL
	1 teaspoon	—	5 mL
	1 tablespoon	—	15 mL
	¼ cup	—	59 mL
	⅓ cup	—	79 mL
	½ cup	—	118 mL
	⅔ cup	—	156 mL
	¾ cup	—	177 mL
	1 cup	—	235 mL
	2 cups or 1 pint	—	475 mL
	3 cups	—	700 mL
	4 cups or 1 quart	—	1 L
	½ gallon	—	2 L
	1 gallon	—	4 L

OVEN TEMPERATURES

FAHRENHEIT	CELSIUS (APPROXIMATE)
250°F	120°C
300°F	150°C
325°F	165°C
350°F	180°C
375°F	190°C
400°F	200°C
425°F	220°C
450°F	230°C

WEIGHT EQUIVALENTS

U.S. STANDARD	METRIC (APPROXIMATE)
½ ounce	15 g
1 ounce	30 g
2 ounces	60 g
4 ounces	115 g
8 ounces	225 g
12 ounces	340 g
16 ounces or 1 pound	455 g

R E F E R E N C E S

"Health Benefits of Seaweed Salad." Nourish by WebMD. Last modified June 22, 2021. webmd.com/diet/health-benefits-seaweed-salad#1.

Saenz, Alissa. "How to Make Seitan." *Connoisseurus Veg.* Last modified August 14, 2018. connoisseurusveg.com/how-to-make-seitan.

Yeh, Tai Sheng, Nu Hui Hung, and Tzu Chun Lin. "Analysis of Iodine Content in Seaweed by GC-ECD and Estimation of Iodine Intake." *Journal of Food and Drug Analysis* 22, no. 2 (June 2014): 189–196. doi.org/10.1016/j.jfda.2014.01.014.

Acknowledgments

Jenni Sekine: Writing a book is a lot harder than I thought it would be. None of this would have been possible without your support, encouragement, and constant reminders to be kind to myself. Thank you for keeping me grounded, giving me feedback on the recipes, and helping me stay focused on the goal. I love you so much, sweetheart!

Nora Sekine: To the best mother a guy could ask for—thank you for everything! I literally wouldn't be here today if it weren't for you. Your strength, patience, and kindness helped me become the man I am today. You taught me how to overcome hurdles in life, how to practice with purpose, and, most important, you showed me how much joy can come from teaching others.

Tyler Sekine: My best friend, my devil's advocate, and my little brother. I suppose you aren't so little anymore, huh? Thank you for being the voice of reason growing up and the source of inspiration for me in our adulthood. I'm proud of you, bro. You are always striving to be better and to take care of our family. You helped keep me motivated while writing this book.

Mateo Baisden: Thank you for being such an awesome mentor. Your patience, understanding, and wisdom were more helpful than you know. I am grateful to call you a friend and I'm excited to share space with you on all the upcoming ventures!

About the Author

BRYAN SEKINE is the founder of Secrets of Sushi, an online resource for teaching people the art of home-made sushi.

Bryan has been a professional sushi chef for more than 13 years, but his passion is in teaching others. He created Secrets of Sushi in 2011 to expand his ability to teach others and has since gone on to teach around the country. At the time of publishing this book, Bryan has taught more than 300 people in his live classes and countless others online. Bryan's goal is to teach people how to make sushi at home, while educating them about the sustainable seafood movement.

For more information on a wide range of sushi topics, recipes, and the sustainable seafood movement, visit SecretsOfSushi.com.